The Life

of Christ

in His

Church

A MISSIOLOGICAL STUDY

OF THE

HISTORY OF THE CHURCH

by

Paul T. Mason, Ph.D.

Thomas P. Neill, Ph.D

Editorial Consultants:

THE REVEREND
Robert W. Argent

THE REVEREND
Charles P. Frankey

THE REVEREND
George H. Frein

THE REVEREND
John J. Hickel

THE REVEREND
William M. Lally

THE REVEREND
Edward T. Moore

THE REVEREND
Paul Search, S.M.

THE REVEREND
John N. Wurm

DANIEL REARDON PUBLISHING COMPANY   CLEVELAND, OHIO

266 ?

Mat

NIHIL OBSTAT: Rt. Rev. William M. Drumm
Censor Librorum

IMPRIMATUR: Joseph Cardinal Ritter
Archbishop of St. Louis
August 6, 1963

Table
of
Contents

I.	The Primitive Period: "Christ Becomes Incarnate in His People"	1
II.	The Church in the Early Middle Ages: "Christ's Body Grows in New People"	27
III.	The Church in the Later Middle Ages: "Christ Shepherds His People"	57
IV.	The Church in the Age of Transition: "Christ Continues to Live in His People"	79
V.	The Age of the Reformation: "Christ Re-creates an Acceptable People"	97
VI.	The Church in an Age of Absolutism: "Christ Abides with His People"	123
VII.	The Church in the Nineteenth Century: "The Body of Christ Comes to New Strength"	145
VIII.	The Contemporary Church: "Christ Remains Faithful to His 'Bride'"	171

The Nature
and Divisions
of Church
History

CHURCH HISTORY is a part of world history, and world history is the story of how men have accepted or refused God's graces. To many people world history seems to be a story of endless confusion and frustration. But to Christians it is the story of salvation, both of the individual person and of mankind.

From the Fall in the Garden of Eden, everything led to the central point of all history: God's personal intervention in history in the person of His Divine Son. This central point is the Redemption of fallen mankind by Christ's life and voluntary death on the cross. History since the time of Christ is essentially the story of the Church's extending the Redemption to all of mankind.

The story concerns itself with the spread of the "good news" of the Gospel to all men, bringing the Light that is Christ to all for whom He died. Our Lord told His disciples: "I am the light of the world. He who follows Me does not walk in the darkness, but will have the light of life." Again He said: "I have come a light into the world, that whoever believes in Me may not remain in the darkness."

Christ told His disciples that they had received this light. "You are the light of the world." They were commissioned to carry this light to the entire world. "I have set thee for a light to the Gentiles," He told them, "to be a means of salvation to the very ends of the earth." Christ gave this commission not only to the twelve Apostles, but to the seventy-two disciples, the *laos* or laity who were the Church. The apostolic commission of spreading the light of the Faith was therefore given to everyone in the Church, and their obligation has always been to spread the Faith through prayer, good works, and missionary effort.

On Pentecost, the birthday of the Church, the Holy Spirit descended on those assembled in the Upper Room in the form of tongues of fire. They emerged from that room full of wisdom and zeal to spread the light of their faith to all men. The story of the Church is the story of its successes and failures to bring the whole world out of darkness and into the light of the Faith.

Each baptized person has played some part, positively or negatively, in this story. In tracing the history of the Church, however, we can pay attention only to the major events and persons in the story. But we must remember that countless Christians participated one way or another in the playing out of this history. Some were valiant in carrying out the commission that Christ gave to all His followers; some were lackadaisical; some failed entirely.

Human and Divine Elements in the Church

The Church is a living organic whole—Christ's Mystical Body. A human body finds the source of its physical life in the natural life-principle that vivifies it—the soul. Similarly, the Church, a supernatural entity, draws supernatural life from the divine life-principle that vivifies it—its Soul, the Holy Spirit; and its Head, Jesus Christ.

This divine life that the Church possesses is spiritual and supernatural and therefore invisible, hidden and full of mystery. But its actions in history are performed by human beings, and therefore there is in them a mingling of the divine life of the Church with human desires and aspirations of the person performing the act. Whenever human beings act, they act under the shadow of sin, for they are subject to the effects of original sin; weakness, ignorance, malice, and error.

Therefore we find in the external manifestations of the Church's life a twofold element: the divine, giving evidence of the supernatural principle from which the fundamental life of the Church springs; and the human, imperfect, natural element—the members of the Church, whose free wills have been allowed by Divine Providence to place limitations on what the infinite, perfect, divine life in the Church can accomplish in the world.

We must remember this so as to understand the problems that we will meet. For we will discover that some popes did not live up to the high moral standards of their office and there have been unworthy bishops, priests, religious, laymen and laywomen. Moreover, we will not be surprised if sometime in our own lives we meet with scandal in the Church, for we will realize that her human members are liable to error, no matter what their calling. Then, although we will grieve over the sin that offends God, still it will not weaken our faith, for we will know the distinction between the Church itself and the members through whom it works.

The Divisions of Church History

Church history is divided into periods or epochs so that we can understand the story more readily. Actually, each period flows into the next and there are no sharp divisions in history. But just as books are divided into chapters for an easier understanding of the subject, so we make the following divisions of Church history:

1) *The primitive period*, during which the Church was founded by Christ and spread, despite persecution,

throughout the Mediterranean area. This Church was a live, vital body of members who were willing to suffer persecutions and death for their Faith. It is in many ways the model toward which leaders in the Church look when they think of reforms to make the Church more perfectly conform to Christ's and His Apostles' intentions.

2) *The Church in the early middle ages,* when the Mystical Body of Christ was challenged by Roman worldliness and the ravages of barbarian invaders. The Church not only survived this troubled time, but converted the barbarians, spread throughout Europe, and shaped a new Christian culture.

3) *The Church in the later middle ages,* in which the Church freed itself from secular control and became in this "Age of Faith" the dominant factor in medieval Europe. In this period the Church became the patron of learning, the mother of universities, and the arbiter of nations. Unfortunately, leaders in the Church began to rely more on their own resources than on the help of the Holy Spirit. Whereas they had formerly spread the light of the Faith by preaching the good news of the Gospel, now they began to rely on the power of the sword. This led to one of the Church's most troubled periods.

4) *The Church in the Age of Transition,* in which the papacy and the Church suffered serious decline. Too much attention was given by Church rulers for a time to worldly affairs and too little to spiritual concerns. Moreover, a secular spirit had developed among men and they became critical of spiritual authorities.

5) *The Age of the Reformation,* which was the result of the conditions that developed in the preceding age. In this period various Protestant groups broke away from the Church and Christendom became religiously fragmented. The Church also reformed itself thoroughly and thus emerged from this period more vigorous and better prepared to carry on its mission than it had been for some time.

6) *The Church in the Age of Absolutism,* in which it enjoyed the support of the government in "Catholic countries," but suffered discrimination or exclusion in other countries. The inner vitality of the Church remained strong in this period and missionary work took on new vigor as European missionaries went in large numbers to the Americas and elsewhere. But the European world became increasingly hostile, as Catholic monarchs tried to make the Church a mere department of the state, and critics of absolutism turned on the Church as well as the state. As the period ended the Church appeared to outsiders as ready to expire.

7) *The Church in the nineteenth century* enjoyed a tremendous revival in the face of an increasingly irreligious world. Saints were numerous, converts were many, missions flourished, spiritual practices multiplied, and sacred learning progressed.

8) *The contemporary Church* enjoys the fruits of the nineteenth century revival. Led by a series of outstanding popes, by excellent bishops and priests, supported by loyal laymen and laywomen who are taking a more active role in the Church's mission of bringing all the world into the light, the Church seems to stand at one of the turning-points in history. It is persecuted in the countries of darkness behind the Iron and Bamboo Curtains, and it faces indifference and hostility among secularminded people in the free Christian world. Nevertheless, it is as strong and vigorous as it has ever been. Missions flourish and spiritual life is healthy. Moreover, modern developments in science and transportation are making it possible for the first time in its history for the Church to be literally and geographically universal by carrying its light into the remotest corners of the earth. The task facing the Church, after two thousand years of carrying out its mission, is more tremendous than ever. But the Church learns, in a human way, from its long history and it seems well equipped to travel the road that lies ahead.

Chapter I

The
Primitive
Period

CHRIST BECOMES INCARNATE
IN HIS PEOPLE

The Founding of the Church

SOMETIME about the year 5 B.C. a Savior was born to the world in Bethlehem. The story is well known to everyone and does not need to be repeated here. But there is an important question. The world had existed many centuries before the coming of Christ and was to exist many more after His coming. Why did God choose to send His Son at that particular time? Only God, of course, can fully answer that question, but St. Paul has given us a hint. He tells us that Christ came "in the fulness of time." That is, that the world was somehow prepared and ready for the coming of the Savior.

The World at the Birth of Christ. At least three important factors help explain in what way the world was prepared. The first of these was political. Astride the

1

Mediterranean world stood the Roman Empire. Due to their great political genius, the Romans had created a political unity and had introduced order. Such order was clearly necessary so that everyone might hear of the teaching of Christ. The second of these factors was cultural. Intellectual and artistic life in the Roman Empire was dominated by the Greek tradition. Everywhere, the educated man spoke Greek. Greek culture thus furnished an intellectual medium in which the teachings of Christianity could be explained. But neither Greek culture nor Roman order could furnish a religious background for Christianity, for religion in the Roman Empire was a curious mixture. Among the common people, paganism was still strong. But its place was being challenged by new and often strange "mystery religions" from the East. At the same time there was a tendency to compromise, to put all religions together into one; a "you worship my gods and I'll worship yours" sort of thing. There was also the new cult of the emperor, which was not so much the worship of a man as it was the worship of the state. Romans believed that the empire was eternal and thus saw it as a fit subject for reverence. Clearly none of these could serve as the religious background for the Christian teaching.

The Jews. The true religious background, the third of our factors, was to be found in Judaism. On the eastern shore of the Mediterranean Sea, in a land called Israel, lived the Jews. Except for a few brief periods they had been politically unimportant, but nonetheless they possessed a special mission. Despite occasional lapses, they had maintained the concept of one true God. Jewish life at the time of Christ, was, however, in a ferment. Roman rule was hated and there were many bloody revolutions. Even Jewish religious life was in difficulty. One group of leaders, known as the Sadducees, had given up many Jewish beliefs in their enthusiasm for Greek philoso-

2

phy. Another and more important group, the Pharisees, avoided all contact with the outside world and insisted on a rigid following of the letter of the mosaic law. Most of the Jews had apparently forgotten the promise of a Savior and even those who remembered expected the coming of a warrior-king to free them from the Romans. Thus, while the Jewish religion formed a suitable religious background, even the Jews themselves were not expecting the coming of the Son of God.

Christ's Teaching. Into such a world Christ was born. As a youth He lived and worked with His parents, Mary and Joseph, in Nazareth, to all outward appearances no different from any other man. But the way was being prepared for Him by John the Baptist and, at about the age of thirty, Jesus began to preach. Christ obviously had some plan in His work. At first, He intended to convert the Jews and thus placed major emphasis on the city of Jerusalem. But almost everywhere He experienced either misunderstanding or opposition. He therefore turned to a small group of followers, His Apostles and disciples. These He would instruct so that they could act as missionaries. Thus, we find in the Gospels accounts of Christ's endless patience in explaining His truth to these humble followers.

The teaching of Christ can be considered under two headings. First, there was His moral teaching. In the Sermon on the Mount, for example, Christ laid down rules of conduct for a true Christian life. At all times He stressed the law of love, the absolute and overriding importance of Charity. To those who would lead the Christian life, He promised eternal salvation. But He did not stop with mere moral exhortation. As God, He knew that man, by himself, was not capable of leading such a life. Man was a social being; he needed a visible institution to aid him. Thus Christ founded His Church. It was to have two major functions. First, it was to teach

3

men and preserve divine truth. Secondly, it was to dispense the sacraments, the source of grace without which a truly Christian life would be impossible. It was commissioned to extend these two functions of teaching and sanctifying to all men of all nations. Hence from the beginning, the Church was to be a missionary church.

The Church. There can be no doubt that the Church which Christ founded was to be a visible one. Time and time again, He spoke of His Kingdom and His Church. Moreover, He gave His Church an organization. The Twelve Apostles, the first bishops, were to govern the Church. To them were given special powers which they were to pass on to their successors. They were to teach and to have charge of the administration of the sacraments. But even the Apostles had their head. This was St. Peter, the first pope, the "rock" upon which the Church was to be built. There were also seventy-two disciples. These "laymen" were also part of Christ's Church. They, too, were His followers and like the Apostles they were commissioned to spread the Faith.

The Passion and Resurrection. But meanwhile, things had come to a head. The Pharisees saw Christ as a danger to their position of leadership and they conspired against Him. The issue was clear. Jesus claimed to be the Son of God and, in the eyes of the Pharisees, this was blasphemy. But in order to execute Him, the power of the Roman government was needed and Pontius Pilate, the governor, was brought into the case. Pilate found himself in an uncomfortable situation, for he believed that Jesus was innocent and yet he feared the power of the Pharisees. While he seemed to be attracted to Jesus, his cynicism held him off. When Jesus told him that "I have come into the world to bear witness to the truth. Everyone who is of the truth hears my voice," Pilate asked, "What is truth?" Christ was thus handed over to the executioners and His passion and death quickly followed.

If this had been the end of the story, the life of Christ would have been of little significance. He would have been merely another moral reformer rejected by an indifferent world too busy for such things. But it was not the end. For on the third day, He rose from the dead. His claim to be God was clearly vindicated.

Christ's Commission to the Apostles. The risen and glorified Christ remained on earth for only forty days. But during this time much was accomplished. Once again He instructed His followers and confirmed the authority of St. Peter as head of the Church. But more importantly, He stressed the essential missionary character of His Church. Shortly before ascending into heaven, He commanded His followers to "Go therefore, and make disciples of all nations, baptizing them in the name of the Father, and of the Son, and of the Holy Spirit, teaching them to observe all that I have commanded you; and behold, I am with you all days, even unto the consummation of the world." His followers were to be no chosen few cutting themselves off from the world. Rather they were to go out into the world, Apostles and disciples, clergy and laymen alike, to spread the truth of Christ.

The Early Expansion of the Faith

It did not take long for the Apostles and disciples to take up the missionary work commanded by Christ. But human effort alone was not sufficient for such a task; divine assistance was clearly needed. Christ had therefore commanded His followers to return to Jerusalem to await the coming of the Holy Spirit.

Pentecost. It was a rather timid and anxious group that gathered in a second story room to wait and pray. Gathered together were the Apostles, Mary, and a great number of disciples. Finally, on the tenth day of their vigil, the promise was fulfilled, and the Holy Spirit descended on them in the form of tongues of fire. The light of the full Faith was theirs. This first Pentecost transformed the followers of Christ into fearless defenders of the Faith. Immediately they began to preach. That same day St. Peter delivered the first sermon and converted some three thousand people.

For some years after this the Apostles apparently remained in Jerusalem and continued to win converts. Because of their success, a conflict with the Jewish leaders was sure to occur and it was not long in coming. Some of the Apostles, including St. Peter, were arrested and commanded to stop their preaching. This did not deter them, however, for St. Peter declared that they would obey God rather than men. Trouble soon became worse. Among the disciples was a certain layman, a deacon named Stephen who had been most vigorous in his preaching and had offended the Jews. As a result, he was stoned to death by a Jewish mob. The martyrdom of St. Stephen was followed by increased persecution. Many of the Apostles were forced to leave Jerusalem and thus began the spread of the Faith to other areas.

St. Paul. Meanwhile, however, the Christians had achieved an important and unexpected victory. Among the most bitter opponents of the Faith was a certain Saul of Tarsus. A man of wide learning, he was a devoted Jew and considered the Christians as traitors to the Jewish religion. But sometime in the year 36 A.D. as Saul was on his way to Damascus to hunt down more Christians, he was knocked from his horse and struck blind. Christ spoke to him and asked, "Saul, Saul, why do you persecute Me?" This statement of our Lord is significant. It reveals the essential truth of the concept of the Church as the mystical body of Christ. To persecute any Christian is in reality to persecute Christ Himself since all are part of this mystical body of which Christ is the Head. As

6

a result of this experience, Saul was converted. His blindness cured, he threw himself into missionary work after having been personally instructed by Christ in the desert. Significantly, St. Paul became the Apostle of the Gentiles.

The Judaizers. A serious problem arose, however, which threatened to curtail the missionary work of the Church. What was the relation of Christianity to Judaism? This question had many practical applications. Most of the early Christians were Jews and they continued to observe Jewish practices along with those of Christianity. Was this really necessary? Moreover, was it necessary to become a Jew before accepting Christianity? Ought the Apostles allow Gentiles to be baptized? Even St. Peter was not, at first, certain. He had hesitated to baptize a Roman centurion named Cornelius, until a vision had instructed him to proceed. Still the problem remained. A group of Jewish Christians, called Judaizers, took a rigid line. They insisted that no Gentile could become a Christian without first accepting Judaism and that Christians must continue to observe the mosaic law. The issue was thus clear and significant, for if Judaism was made a prerequisite for accepting Christianity the task of converting all nations would become almost impossible. If the Church was to become truly universal the position of the Judaizers had to be rejected.

The Council of Jerusalem. In the year 49 A.D. the Apostles Peter, Paul, James, and John met to discuss the problem. This was the Council of Jerusalem, the first council of the Church. James, the Bishop of Jerusalem, defended the Judaizer position, while Paul led the opposition. The final decision, however, rested with St. Peter, the head of the Church. Finally, Peter announced his decision. Gentiles, he said, could become Christians without first accepting Judaism. Moreover, even Jewish Christians were no longer bound to the mosaic law. The

Church was thus freed from its complete dependence on Judaism. It was to be truly universal, as Christ had intended, and to spread to the whole world.

Missionary Activity.　The missionary work of the Church now became extensive. The work of St. Paul was especially important. Between 53 and 57 A.D. he traveled throughout Asia Minor and even made an attempt to convert the Greeks at Athens. Everywhere, his method was the same. First, he approached the Jewish community and was usually rejected. Then he turned to the Gentiles, often achieving striking success. St. Paul also took care to provide for the continued life of the churches that he founded. In every community he appointed followers to watch over the church and he wrote many letters or Epistles to guide them. St. Paul was later arrested and taken to Rome but after the year 63 A.D. he made more journeys into Asia Minor and also into the western part of the Empire, going perhaps as far as Spain. Sometime between the years 64 and 67 A.D. Paul was put to death in the city of Rome.

St. Peter, too, was active. His early travels are obscure but it is certain that he went to Rome, made many converts, and became the first bishop of the city. He, too, was put to death at the same time as St. Paul. The activities of the other Apostles are not so clear. St. James, the Bishop of Jerusalem, also suffered martyrdom. St. John, the youngest of the Apostles, often suffered persecution but lived until about the year 100 A.D. when he died a natural death in Asia Minor. Very early tradition held that St. Thomas went to India, St. Bartholomew to Persia, St. Philip to Phrygia, St. Matthew to Ethiopia, St. Andrew to Scythia, and St. Thaddeus to Edessa.

Just how many converts were made in these early years is unknown but their number must have been considerable. Probably every part of the Mediterranean world was touched in some way by the Christian message by the end of the first century. Many factors were important in this remarkable expansion of the Faith. Clearly, the guiding hand of the Holy Spirit was most important. The dedication of the early Christians to missionary work was also of great significance. Finally, the high moral principles of the Faith, its stress on love, and its doctrine of salvation had a compelling effect on the minds of men. The beauty and truth of Christianity must have been apparent to many who could no longer find hope in a decaying paganism.

Sacred Writings. The Apostolic Age was a period of an expanding Christian literature. The Gospels of Matthew, Mark, Luke, and John were written and known by the early Christians. These divinely inspired works recounted the life of Christ, but more importantly they recorded the teachings of Christ so that all would have a sure guide to the Faith. At about the same time, St. Luke wrote the *Acts of the Apostles* which are of great historical value for showing us the early life of the Church. There were also the many Epistles written by the different Apostles to churches which they had founded. These, too, were a source of divine revelation. With the writing of the *Apocalypse* by St. John, the New Testament was finished and with the death of St. John, the last Apostle, the store of divine public revelation entrusted to the Church was complete.

The Hierarchy. What of the organization of the Church in these early years? Already the distinction between the clergy and the laity was apparent, as it had been during the life of Christ. Moreover, a hierarchy existed within the clergy itself. The Apostles passed on their spiritual powers to their successors, the bishops. In every city where a Christian community existed there was a bishop responsible for preserving the true doctrine and dispensing the sacraments. Under the bishops were priests who,

9

with the permission of the bishops, might also dispense the sacraments. Deacons, too, existed, who were responsible for caring for the material needs of the people. In some areas there were catecists who instructed prospective converts in the essentials of the Faith. But there was one who stood above all these. This was the bishop of Rome, the successor of St. Peter, and the visible head of the Church.

The Liturgy. The liturgy, of course, was much simpler than it is today but all the sacraments were used. Baptism was most important and was usually administered by the bishop. A form of Ordination was also used for the purpose of preparing new clergy. The Mass, too, was celebrated at least every Sunday, although it did not usually take place in anything like a present day church. Usually, the faithful gathered in a private home where, after the eating of a common meal, prayers were said, bread and wine were consecrated, and all partook of the sacrament of Holy Communion.

In every respect, the life of these Christian communities was marked by that charity commanded by Christ. Slavery, for example, was not forbidden but masters were commanded to treat their slaves fairly and to provide for their spiritual welfare. Quite often, too, these Christian communities practiced a sort of primitive communism, holding all their property in common and allowing it to be administered for the good of all by the bishop with the help of the deacons. It was, indeed, this charity which represented the most attractive and compelling aspect of Christianity in the eyes of the pagans.

The Church in Conflict

It was inevitable that Christianity would sooner or later come into conflict with the Roman Empire, for paganism was the official religion of the state. Moreover, Christianity was something new and men, even modern

men, usually distrust new things which they do not understand. As the number of Christians grew, therefore, the
possibility of trouble grew proportionately.

Causes of the Persecutions. Romans were not an in-
tolerant people, rather, their known toleration of various
peoples and customs was one of the chief factors in their
political success. But Rome expected something of its
subjects which Christians would not give. Rome was
willing to let anyone worship whatever gods he might
choose as long as he would also agree to worship the
Roman emperor, the symbol of the state. This the Christians would not do. Thus they were accused of treason
and atheism. But persecution was not solely the work of
the government. Public opinion, too, condemned the
Christians. The educated and the wealthy saw the new
religion as the refuge of the riff-raff and the low born,
and consequently feared and despised it. Even ordinary
people were mistrustful of the Christians. Because Christian services were usually held in secrecy, rumors soon
began to circulate that horrible deeds—even cannibalism
—were part of the ceremonies. Moreover, because of the
low moral standards of the day, Christians could not
attend the public amusements. Neither the cruelty of the
Roman sports nor the obscenity of the Roman theater
were fit for Christian attendance. But the ordinary Roman
did not understand such behavior. His religion made no
such demands on him and he looked upon Christians as
anti-social and often called them "haters of the human
race."

Early Persecutions. The first persecution broke out during the reign of the emperor Nero (54-68 A.D.). A great
fire swept through Rome and the Christians were naturally blamed for it. Nero immediately began a bitter
persecution during which both St. Peter and St. Paul
perished. From that time on, Christianity was forbidden

11

by the state. Persecution was not yet, however, a constant thing; periods of bitter repression were followed by years of comparative peace.

Position of the Roman Government.   During the reign of Trajan (98-112 A.D.) the position of the Roman government became clear. Pliny the Younger, the governor of a Roman province, wrote to the emperor for instructions on how to deal with the Christians. Trajan replied that the state should not directly seek out Christians. But, he said, Christianity was a crime and if a private citizen accused someone of practicing Christianity, the state would have to take action. If the accused denied he was a Christian or gave us his Faith by worshipping the emperor he was to be released, otherwise he was to be executed. As a result of this policy; several persecutions occurred in the second century, most of them brought on by public demand. The number who perished is not known but among the victims were at least three popes.

Attitude of the Christians.   What was the reaction of the Christians to these persecutions? While many gave up their Faith in fear of their lives, the majority remained faithful despite the cost. They remained, in fact, quite moderate. They did not openly seek or invite persecution, as the fanatic would have done, but rather met it quietly when it was forced upon them. Nor were they revolutionaries. They did not revolt against the emperor, nor seek to overthrow the state. Instead, they observed the laws of the state whenever these did not contradict their Faith and many even served in the Roman armies. In general, they attempted to follow the command of Christ to "render to Caesar the things that are Caesar's and to God the things that are God's."

But the Christians did not remain completely passive. Even in the midst of persecution they sought to spread Christianity and to make known the justice of their cause. A group of men known as the Second Century Apologists, such as St. Justin Martyr, stepped forward to explain and defend the Faith. They pointed out the absurdity of the Roman position. Was it not ridiculous, they asked, to treat Christianity as a crime and then punish it only if a private citizen complained? Moreover, if Christianity was truly a crime why was the accused released simply because he denied the charge or gave up his Faith? Why did the state not attempt to prove the charges as it did in the case of murderers or robbers? But the Apologists did not stop here. They asked how men whose lives were as upright and blameless as the Christians could be criminals? They also attempted to convert the Romans by their writings. Many appeals were addressed to the emperors themselves in the hope of gaining their favor. Other writings explained the Faith in such a way as to attract the educated upper classes.

Later Persecutions. But the persecutions did not end and the third century was an extremely troubled era. Years of peace were followed by terrible suffering. At times, certain of the emperors seemed to be favorable to the Christians and one, Philip the Arabian (243-249 A.D.), was thought to be a Christian. The danger, however, was far from over. The state was slowly becoming more active and was beginning to take steps to root out and punish Christians. Thus a particularly severe persecution broke out after the year 251 A.D. under the emperors Decius and Valerian. This, however, was followed by another few years of peace.

The final great assault on the Church was made during the reign of the emperor Diocletian (284-305 A.D.), one of the most powerful of the Roman emperors. At first he had been favorable to the Faith, but a series of unfortunate incidents turned him into a bitter persecutor. A series of imperial decrees ordered the destruction of all Christian churches and the arrest of the clergy. A final edict, issued in 304 A.D., commanded that every citizen throughout the empire must make a sacrifice to

13

the emperor to prove his paganism. The state was now actively seeking out Christians and, as a result, this persecution was the most terrible of all. Many apostatized or denied Christ. But the Church was not destroyed, and after the death of Diocletian in 305 A.D. the persecution died down. Christianity was growing stronger and gaining more converts. The time of its victory over the Roman Empire was close at hand.

Christian Life. The persecutions undoubtedly had a tremendous effect on Christianity, but they did not completely disrupt Christian life. The charity which everywhere marked a Christian did not disappear. Even the pagans noticed the love which Christians bore to each other and to their God. They were impressed by the Christians' willingness to meet death for their Faith and many conversions resulted from such courage.

During the persecutions, the catacombs, long underground passages, became important to the Christians. Here they buried their dead and often carried out their sacred services. Here, too, the beginnings of a beautiful Christian art were to be found. Another result of the persecutions was that Christian morals became unusually severe. In some churches confession was public rather than private and, in some instances, the performance of the penance was required before the granting of absolution. But such severity was often a help to the Christian who not only had to prepare himself to face death, but also had to steel himself against the temptations of a worldly Roman society. The liturgy was also being developed. Feasts such as Christmas, Easter, and the remembrance of the martyrs and saints such as St. Peter, St. Paul, and the Blessed Mother were commonly observed.

Early Theologians. The Faith also produced great thinkers during these centuries of persecution. St. Irenaeus of Lyons (140-202 A.D.), perhaps the first true theologian, defended and explained Christianity in his many writings. At the same time, Tertullian (155-220 A.D.) did much to develop a needed Latin terminology for theology. While he later fell into heresy, his work was of immense importance. St. Cyprian of Carthage (d. 258 A.D.) defended the authority of the bishops against heretics and although he fell into a serious quarrel with the papacy, he died in communion with Rome. Finally, there was Origen (185-253 A.D.) who was, perhaps, the most brilliant of them all. While he made certain errors, he wrote on every aspect of the Faith and had some two thousand works to his credit. Thus, even in the midst of persecution, the basis of a Christian theology was prepared.

The Christian Victory

Constantine. Early in the fourth century a bitter civil war was being waged throughout the Roman world. Diocletian had divided the Empire into four areas, each with its own ruler. But as might have been expected, each of the four was determined to gain complete control. One of the contestants was Constantine, the ruler of what is today France and England, and a man who, as his father before him, was tolerant towards Christianity. Then, shortly before the battle of the Milvian Bridge, which was to decide his fate, Constantine saw a cross in the sky with the inscription "In this sign conquer." As a result, he had the shields of his soldiers marked with the sign of the cross and won a great victory over his rival, Maxentius. Constantine was now the master of the entire Western Empire and he announced his intention of becoming a Christian. The result was that Christianity was no longer to be persecuted. In the year 313 A.D. Constantine and Licinius, the ruler of the Eastern Empire, issued the *Edict of Milan,* granting full toleration to the Faith. The Church also regained much of the property which had been lost during the persecution. Constantine

15

was not, however, a model Christian. His personal life left much to be desired and he did not accept baptism until he was at the point of death. Furthermore, he retained the title of Pontifex Maximus—that is, chief priest of the pagan cult. Paganism still remained the official religion of the Roman Empire.

The immediate successors of Constantine took steps to promote Christianity and weaken the hold of paganism. Quite naturally many Romans were offended, because paganism was not only a religious matter, but was also tied in with Roman patriotism. Thus, there was a movement to end the influence of Christianity within the Empire.

The Pagan Reaction. This attempt came to a head during the reign of the emperior Julian (361-363 A.D.). Although he is often called Julian the Apostate, the name does not really apply, for he had never been a Christian. Instead, he was devoted to Greek philosophy and paganism. Thus he sought to stamp out Christianity and strengthen the pagan religion. But Julian's effort was a failure. In 363 A.D. he was killed on the field of battle and his last words, so tradition has it, were "Galilean (Jesus Christ), Thou hast conquered."

Christianity Established. After the death of Julian the growth of Christian influence continued. The emperor Gratian (375-383 A.D.), himself a Christian, renounced the title of Pontifex Maximus and deprived paganism of any financial support from the state. Finally, the emperor Theodosius I (379-395 A.D.) declared Christianity the official religion of the Roman Empire, and forbade all public pagan sacrifices. But paganism did not cease to exist, for there were no persecutions of individual pagans, and especially in the countryside the old superstitions held on for a long time. However, Christianity had clearly triumphed.

Church and State. The conquest of the Roman Empire was not an unmixed blessing. To be sure, Christians were happy that the emperors had accepted their religion, but a Christian emperor presented many problems. What was his position within the Church? How could a man who enjoyed unlimited political power be a humble subject of his bishop? Moreover, what was the relation between the spiritual power of the Church and the temporal power of the state? Christ had, of course, provided an answer: "Render to Caesar the things that are Caesar's and to God the things that are God's." The Church, then, was superior in all spiritual affairs and the state was supreme in all temporal affairs. But when was a thing spiritual and when was it temporal, and what if it was both? Who then should have the final word? While the Church held that in the case of a conflict it should make the final decision, this was not always followed. Occasionally, emperors paid no attention to Church teaching. Occasionally, also, they intervened in purely spiritual questions. Often when disputes broke out over Christian dogma, emperors proved willing to compromise the truth in order to prevent a political disturbance. Also, Christians intervened in purely temporal affairs. In 388 A.D., for example, a Christian mob burned a Jewish synagogue and when the emperor Theodosius ordered them to pay for the damages, St. Ambrose denounced him and forced him to withdraw the order. But despite all these difficulties, Church and state usually managed to work together for the welfare of all.

Church Organization. The conquest of the Roman Empire had other important effects. When the persecutions ended, the Church came into the open and perfected her organization. The basic unit was still the bishopric. Almost every city had its bishop with a number of clergy under him. Moreover, the clergy were more and more following the practice of celibacy. The bish-

17

oprics themselves were grouped into provinces each presided over by an archbishop. Among these archbishops were also a number of Patriarchs, bishops, who, because of the importance of their cities, enjoyed an unusual prestige. Among these were the Patriarchs of Antioch, Jerusalem, Alexandria, and especially the Patriarch of Constantinople, the new capital of the Empire.

But the Patriarch of Rome, the pope, was the true ruler of the Church. He and he alone had the power to make the final decision with regard to the teaching of the Church. While there were times when certain bishops opposed the views of the pope, his power was clearly recognized. St. Irenaeus of Lyons, for example, pointed out that to be truly Christian one must conform to the teaching of Rome.

The victory also had its effect on Christian practices. The Mass was now celebrated at an altar in beautiful churches. At least every Sunday the bishop, attended by his clergy, offered the Holy Sacrifice, and the faithful received the Body and Blood of our Lord. At the same time, Christian morals lost some of their former severity. Yet charity and dedication to the Faith still remained the dominant characteristic of a Christian.

Missionary Efforts. The end of the persecutions also served to increase the missionary efforts of the Church. Free to practice their faith openly, Christians now sought to convert everyone within the Empire. It is estimated that during the life of Constantine only ten percent of the population was Christian. But this number was rapidly increased. All parts of the Empire experienced a growth in the number of Christians, and lands as far away as Arabia felt the impact of the teaching of Christ.

Heresy and the Development of Christian Doctrine

During the same centuries when the Church was experiencing the opposition of the Roman state, she was also undergoing great internal difficulties. The most serious of these was the growth of heresy. Heresy may be defined as any teaching or belief which contradicts the teaching of the Church, the true teaching of Christ and His Apostles.

There were many factors which led to the growth of heresy. Among them was the fact that there were a great number of religious ideas in the Roman Empire, many of them superstitious, and there was the danger that these would become mixed up with true Christian doctrine. Indeed, many people made this mistake. There was also a danger from Greek and Roman philosophy, for in an attempt to explain the Faith to the intellectual classes there was the possibility that Christianity would be compromised. The greatest cause of heresy, however, was simply the attempt of men to understand and explain more completely the doctrines of the Church.

The essential truths of the Christian religion had all been stated by Christ and His Apostles, but men wished to better understand and explain these truths by the use of their reason. There was, however, always the danger of error in such reasoning, for many of the Christian doctrines are mysteries—that is, they can never be fully understood by man. Often, sufficient caution was not observed. In an anxiety to stress the fact that Christ was truly God, for example, certain thinkers were apt to forget that He was also truly man. Such mistakes, in themselves, were to be expected and would have caused little trouble. The difficulty came when some men, motivated by intellectual pride, refused to listen to the warnings of the Church and continued to hold their erroneous opinions.

Early Heresies.   Certain heresies arose quite early in the history of the Church. These were called "Syncretic" heresies, for influenced by the Roman trend known as syncretism, they sought to combine a great number of

19

other religious and philosophical ideas with the teachings of the Church.

The most important of these early heresies was known as *Gnosticism*. It held that certain men have a special knowledge (a *Gnosis*) which comes directly from God. This special knowledge guaranteed to those who possessed it certain salvation. Moreover, the Gnostics held, it was superior to the teaching of the Church. Even the power of the sacraments amounted to little in comparison with the Gnosis. Thus Gnosticism was a serious danger, for it definitely contradicted the teaching of Christ and undermined the authority of the Church. But despite the fact that Christian writers repeatedly warned of its dangers, the heresy remained a serious menace throughout those early centuries.

Other heresies soon arose which were very similar to Gnosticism. One of these was *Marcionism*, founded by a certain Marcion in the second century. Marcion denied that the God of the Jews was the same as the Christian God. Thus, he changed the Bible, throwing out the entire Old Testament and keeping only the Gospel of St. Luke and the Epistles of St. Paul in the New Testament. Marcion even attempted to organize his own church complete with bishops and clergy.

Another heresy was known as *Montanism*. Its founder, Montanus, who lived in the second century, claimed that the end of the world was near and with a group of followers he went into the mountains to await the second coming of our Lord. Although the world failed to end, he still insisted that private revelation was superior to the teaching of the Church.

Finally, there was the heresy known as *Manicheaism*, taught by a certain Mani, a Persian who lived in the third century. Mani held that there were two gods, not one: a god of evil and a god of good. The creation of the world had been the work of the evil god and thus all material and wordly things were evil. Christ, then, the representative of the good god, was not truly human.

All of these early heresies not only contradicted the true teaching of the Church, but they were also excessively severe in their morality. They believed that all material pleasures were evil and even marriage was denounced as sinful. Doctrines such as this were far more serious than completely immoral doctrines because they tended to destroy God's plan for the world. But despite their false teachings these heresies found many supporters and were a serious danger to the Church. Even Tertullian, the great theologian, fell away from the Church and became a Montanist in his later life. But more serious heresies were soon to arise.

Disciplinary Heresies. The later heresies were of two kinds. The first of these were "disciplinary" heresies; that is, false teachings about morality and Christian practice and discipline. Among such heretical groups were the *Novations.* They held that any Christian who denies his Faith commits an unforgivable sin which cannot be absolved even by the sacrament of Penance. Now the early Church, as we have seen, was very strict about the forgiveness of sins, but the Novations went too far. Their doctrine contradicted the plain teaching of Christ that any sin can be forgiven if the sinner is truly sorry and is determined to lead a good life in the future.

Another group, the *Donatists,* held that a sacrament given by a bishop or priest who is in the state of mortal sin is not valid. This was an especially serious error, for it would have undermined the whole sacramental system of the Church. A man going to confession, for example, could never be sure that his sins had been forgiven, since it is always possible that the priest who absolved him was not in the state of grace.

Finally, there was a group known as *Pelagians.* They

denied original sin and taught that man, without the aid of divine grace, could achieve salvation. This again was a dangerous doctrine, for it, too, taught that the sacraments were unnecessary.

Christological Heresies. More serious, however, were the *Christological* heresies, or false teachings about Christ. The Trinity, of course, is a mystery because no one can fully understand how there can be three Persons in one God. Moreover, there is a mystery connected with the Second Person of the Trinity. How can Christ be both truly man and truly God? It was out of such questions and problems that these heresies arose.

The first of these was *Arianism* derived from the teachings of a certain Arius who lived in the early fourth century. Arius held that Christ was not truly God, but rather that He was only a very special creature of God. Arianism was a very serious heresy, because if Christ was not God His death on the cross could not atone for the sins of man. But it made many converts and caused much unrest within the Church. Certain of the emperors (including Constantine who was baptized by an Arian priest) adopted the heresy and tried to impose it upon the faithful.

Those attempting to refute Arianism sometimes fell into other errors equally as serious. *Nestorianism,* which arose in the fifth century was an example of this. Nestorius wished to save both the humanity and the divinity of Christ, but he went too far. He held that Christ was really two persons. Thus, he denied that Mary was truly the Mother of God; she was simply the mother of Christ's human person. This teaching provoked a great controversy and once again there were serious splits within the Church.

Again, in an attempt to fight Nestorianism, a new heresy arose. This was *Monophysitism.* The Monophysites taught that Christ was indeed only one Person, but they made the mistake of holding that Christ's human nature was completely absorbed in His divine nature. The result of this view was that Christ was not really human. The dispute had now gone full circle. The Arians had started by denying that Christ was truly God. The Nestorians had denied that Christ was one person. Finally, the Monophysites had denied that Christ was truly human.

Church Councils. But what was the reaction of the Church to all these heresies? How was the truth upheld in the midst of so much confusion? Church councils were one means of defense. Here many of the bishops of the Chruch met together, and under the guidance of the Papacy they preserved Christian truth by defining and upholding the teaching of Christ.

The first great council was held at Nicaea in the year 325 A.D. The Arian heresy was condemned and the divinity of Christ was upheld. At the same time, the famous *Nicaean Creed* was formulated. But, as has been seen, other heresies soon arose. In 431 A.D. the great Council of Ephesus convened to combat Nestorianism. The defenders of Nestorius refused to participate and it was a long time before the heresy could be condemned.

The attempt to deal with Monophysitism caused even greater difficulty. A council in 449 A.D., known as the "Robber Council," paid no attention to the Papacy, refused to condemn the heresy, and even persecuted defenders of the Faith. To make matters worse, the emperor Theodosius supported the heretics. Finally, however, the issue was settled. In 451 A.D. the Council of Chalcedon listened to the instructions of Pope Leo the Great and condemned the Monophysite heresy. The true Christian teaching was defined. Christ was one Person in Whom there were both human and divine natures. Heresy did not, of course, completely end. Disputes were many, but the Church had nonetheless upheld true Christian doctrine.

Church Fathers. Another important factor in the battle against heresy was the work of great Christian thinkers. These men are known as "Fathers of the Church." Among the more important of them in the East were St. Athanasius and St. Basil, both of whom were fearless foes of Arianism. There was also St. John Chrysostom who suffered persecution because of his opposition to the Monophysite heresy. In the West, there were many important Fathers. St. Jerome (347-419 A.D.) translated the Bible into Latin. St. Ambrose, Bishop of Milan from 374 to 397 A.D., defended the Church from the unlawful claims of emperors to intervene in spiritual matters.

Finally, there was St. Augustine (354-430 A.D.). As a young man he was a Manichean and led an immoral life, but he later accepted Christianity and became one of its strongest defenders. As Bishop of Hippo in North Africa, he battled against heresy and, as a result of his many writings, became the greatest theologian of the early Church.

Fortunately, then, the Church withstood the threat of heresy. Heresy could have destroyed the Mystical Body of Christ, because such teachings and unnaturally severe morals contradicted the wisdom of Christ. But, on the other hand, heresy played an important part in the development of Christian doctrine. The fact that mistakes were made forced the defenders of the Faith to understand better and define more clearly the true Christian teaching. In this way Christian theology was born.

Conclusion

We have now examined the history of the early Church. It is an unprecedented story of success. Beginning with a small group of Apostles and disciples the

Church had spread throughout the Western civilized world and had conquered the Roman Empire. Moreover, it had withstood the internal threats of heresy. What could account for such amazing success? The guiding hand of the Holy Spirit was, of course, most important. But in human affairs God ordinarily works through men. The early Christians did not fail Him. They accepted the commission of Christ to teach and baptize all nations. By their willingness to face death and to live a truly Christian life, they brought the message of Christ to the world and infused civilization with a new spirit.

STUDY QUESTIONS

1. What is Christ's message to men?
2. What was the first of the wonderful deeds of God for His people in the history of the Church?
3. Contrast the Church of this age as viewed by the pagan and by the Christian.
4. In what way was the life of the Church in the first century like the earthly life of Christ?
5. Describe the early persecutions of the Church of God as providential events.
6. Describe the mentality of the Christian martyr.
7. Why did heresy arise in the early Church and how did it lead to a better understanding of the message of Christ?
8. Why would the Christians in the first century of the history of the Church look upon their age as the end of history?
9. In what sense is the Church of the first century an organization and in what sense is it more than an organization? Illustrate your answer.
10. What is the meaning of the subtitle to this chapter, "Christ Becomes Incarnate in His Church"? Explain doctrinally and illustrate historically.

25

Bibliography

DeWohl, Louis. *Glorious Folly: A Novel of the Time of St. Paul.* (New York: 1957).

———. *The Restless Flame: A Novel of St. Augustine.* (Philadelphia: 1951).

(The above two books are very readable, somewhat fictionalized accounts of two of the great leaders of the early Church.)

Jones, Arnold H. M. *Constantine and the Conversion of Europe.* (New York: 1949).

(A good study of the emperor who granted toleration to Christianity.)

The New Testament.

(This is the basic source for the early history of the Church. It should be read by every student of the history of the Church.)

O'Brien, Isidore. *The Life of Christ.* (Paterson, N.J.: 1944).

(A rather short life of Christ.)

———. *Peter and Paul, Apostles: An Account of the Early Years of the Church.* (Paterson, N.J.: 1950).

(A good account of two of the Apostles.)

Prat, Ferdinand. *Jesus Christ: His Life, His Teaching, and His Work.* 2 vols. Translated by John J. Herman, S.J. (Milwaukee: 1958).

(A longer and more advanced study of the life of Christ.)

Walsh, William Thomas. *St. Peter, The Apostle.* (New York: 1948).

(A good biography of the first Pope.)

Chapter **II**

The Church in the Early Middle Ages

CHRIST'S BODY GROWS IN NEW PEOPLE

Introduction

CHRISTIANITY had conquered the Roman Empire and Christians undoubtedly looked forward to long years of co-operation between the Church and the Roman state. Such, however, was not to be the case, for within a few years after the establishment of Christianity, the barbarian invasions began and the Roman Empire crumbled to pieces. The centuries which followed—the fifth to the eleventh—were not easy ones. They have, in fact, often been called the "Dark Ages." But the Church rose to the challenge. It survived the invasions and eventually converted the barbarians. It preserved civilization and the cultural heritage of the ancient world. But it also experienced grave difficulties and troubles. The story of this chapter, then, is the story of the Church in a troubled era. But it is also the story of the Church shaping that era, emerging victorious from it, and establishing Christianity throughout all of Europe.

The Barbarian Invasions

The Decline of Rome. When Theodosius established Christianity as the official religion of Rome, the Empire was already in serious trouble. The hold of the imperial government was slowly breaking down. Moreover, Rome's dependence on slavery had weakened the economic life of the Empire. Even more serious was the moral and intellectual decay of the Roman world. The excessive love of pleasure had taken the inevitable toll. Divorce and birth control were widespread and as a result the population of the Empire declined seriously. In the midst of such circumstances only the slightest shock was needed to shatter the entire structure and that shock was the barbarian invasions.

The Barbarian Invasions. Outside the boundaries of the Roman Empire lived many tribes of semi-civilized Germans and Slavs. These so-called barbarians led a nomadic existence and they were attracted by the wealth and splendor of the Roman Empire. For centuries small numbers had drifted into the Empire, became Romanized, and usually joined the Roman army. But in the latter part of the fourth century German barbarians were attacked by wild, swift-riding Huns who swept out of the steppes of Asia. The German barbarians rolled back under these attacks and fled by the thousands into the helpless Roman Empire.

Various barbarian kingdoms were set up within the crumbling ruins of the Roman Empire, which they had overrun and destroyed. The Empire ceased to exist and in its place stood a number of barbarian kingdoms. The Church would soon feel the effects of such a radical transformation of political power.

Effects on the Church. Christians, like all other Romans, were devoted to the Roman Empire and its political institutions. "When Rome falls," St. Jerome stated, "the world falls." Moreover, because the barbarians in their search for gold and precious gems often plundered and pillaged churches, Christians had good reason to fear the newcomers.

At the same time, however, the coming of the barbarians opened up a whole new field of missionary activity. Christians soon realized that the invaders could not be ignored; it would be necessary to convert them. This, however, was no easy task. It would not have been so difficult, perhaps, had the barbarians still been pagan. Many of them, however, had already been converted to Christianity by the missionary Ulfilias (311-383). But unfortunately Ulfilias was an Arian and the barbarians had accepted an heretical version of Christianity. Thus, they looked upon true Christians as enemies. The result was persecution. In Spain the Visigoths tried to convert all to Arianism and in North Africa the Vandals were especially cruel in attacking Christians. Even in Italy, the capable Theodoric forbade his subjects to have any dealings at all with the native Christians. The task of conversion, then, was not to be an easy one.

The Church also had the responsibility of preserving civilization, for with the Empire in decay only the Church remained as the guardian of culture and knowledge. The great work of the Church in this respect was well symbolized by Pope St. Leo the Great (440-461). During his reign the Huns were preparing to attack the city of Rome. The Roman Senate did nothing. Rather, it was Pope Leo who went outside the city walls and persuaded the conqueror to spare the city.

In the final analysis, Christians might indeed mourn that the Empire had fallen. They might indeed tremble at the task before them, but they could also derive hope from the fact that the Church, founded by God, had withstood and would soon conquer a force that had destroyed the greatest achievement of ancient civilization, the Roman Empire.

Monasticism

One of the agencies by which the Church preserved itself and spread the Faith was *monasticism*. Monasticism may be defined as a way of life in which Christians withdraw from the world and devote themselves to the sole task of serving Christ and saving their souls. The practice of mortification and the complete dedication of one's life to God had always existed in the Church. Christ had recommended and strongly encouraged such a life. But in the beginning there was no formal organization; men and women practiced their mortifications at home.

Early Monasticism. The practice of monasticism first began in the East. Holy men and women simply withdrew from the world and lived the life of a hermit in some secluded spot, often in the desert. There was no rule, no superior, and no community life, although occasionally a group of such hermits might gather for sacred services. Usually, the mortifications practiced by such men were extremely severe. St. Simeon Stylites (d.459), for example, chained himself to a rock, and, after being commanded by his bishop to abandon that practice, spent the rest of his life on a tiny platform thirty feet in the air. St. Anthony of Egypt (d.356) was the great exponent of such a life and he provided spiritual direction to a great number of like-minded disciples.

This early kind of hermit life or as it is called, Anchorite Monasticism, was obviously not suited for everyone. The rigors of such a life were too severe for all but the heartiest and there were many abuses. Monks came and went as they pleased and there were always temptations to laxity or overseverity. Thus, the idea of a more formal kind of monasticism soon arose.

Cenobitic Monasticism. In this later type of monasticism there was a communal life; several monks began to live together. Moreover, a rule of conduct and a daily routine of life were usually established. Generally too, there was a superior to rule over the monks and to act as their spiritual adviser. The real founder of Cenobitic monasticism was St. Pachomius (290-345). A native of Egypt, he acted as the head of some nine monasteries and composed a rule for them. It provided for a superior, a waiting period before admission to the monastic life, and a very severe discipline.

St. Basil the Great (329-379), however, brought monasticism in the East to its greatest heights. His rule was notable for its moderation. Moreover, it provided for a balance between work and prayer, and encouraged the study of Holy Scripture. It was so successful that even to the present day, the Basilian Rule has remained dominant in the East.

Early Western Monasticism. Monasticism did not develop solely in the East. Very soon a strong movement was flourishing in the West. St. Jerome and St. Ambrose, both Fathers of the Church, were early exponents of the monastic life. So was St. Augustine. As Bishop of Hippo he set up religious houses for both men and women and a letter to one of these soon became the basis of a monastic rule. In France there was a strong development under St. Hilary, St. Martin of Tours, and Blessed John Cassian. Ireland, too, was the seat of an especially vigorous monastic life after St. Patrick had converted the country. But these were only steps in the right direction. These early attempts were too closely modeled on the East, and Eastern forms were not suited to either the climate or the conditions of Western life. A truly native form of Western monasticism was clearly needed.

St. Benedict of Nursia (480-547) was the true founder of Western monasticism. Born of a good family and educated in Rome, he decided as a youth to devote himself fully to God. Soon famous for his great piety he attracted a large number of disciples and established his first monastery at Monte Cassino, south of Rome. Here he composed his great rule.

The Benedictine rule is noted for its moderation. In the prologue, Benedict wrote that "We must form a school of divine service in which nothing too heavy or too rigorous will be established." The monks were to eat and sleep sufficiently to maintain health and even meat and wine were allowed in moderate amounts. The abbot was warned not to allow the most dedicated of the monks to set the standards for all. Benedict also provided for public vows of poverty, chastity, obedience, and stability. No longer were monks allowed to come and go as the mood struck them. A government was also provided. The monks were to elect an abbot whose authority was to be unquestioned, except that all were to be subject to the bishop. The life of the monks was to revolve around the three duties of prayer, spiritual reading, and manual labor, for Benedict was determined that his monasteries should be self-sufficient and that the monks should provide for themselves. The rule established by St. Benedict soon spread to all the West, winning acceptance everywhere.

Significance of Monasticism. The development of monasticism was of immense importance to the Faith and to civilization as well. Even though the primary objective of the monks was simply to save their own souls, they nevertheless performed numerous services. They took care of the poor and maintained hospitals and schools. They were very active in agriculture and through their efforts much new land was cleared and brought under cultivation. Under the influence of Cassiodorus (475-570) they soon turned to the copying of ancient manuscripts and it is chiefly due to their work that many ancient writings were preserved. Moreover, they provided the Church with capable leaders, for monks were often called upon to be bishops and popes. Most important of all, however, their efforts were decisive in the conversion of the West. More than any other group the monks were responsible for carrying the word of God to the barbarians and the establishment of churches throughout Europe.

The Conversion of the West

The problem presented to the Church by the barbarians was a serious one. Previously the Church had expanded within the confines and culture of the Roman Empire. Now the Church was forced to cope with people who were either pagans or Arians, and who did not understand the Roman way of life. Christ, however, had intended His Church to be universal and the missionary work of the Church soon overcame all obstacles to the conversion of the barbarians.

Ireland. The great work of spreading the Faith began in Ireland even before the barbarian invasions. St. Patrick (385-461) was born in England, then under Roman rule, and was raised a Christian. At the age of sixteen, however, he was carried away to Ireland by a band of pirates. Though he had been only a lukewarm believer, his sufferings in captivity transformed him into a sincere and dedicated Christian. By the time he escaped from Ireland in 407 he had so well mastered the doctrine of Christian love that he determined to return to the island in order to spread the gospel.

Before doing so, however, he went to France to prepare himself both spiritually and intellectually and while there he became a monk. Then, in 432, he returned to Ireland. His success was amazing. By concentrating on winning the favor of native chieftains he managed to convert practically the entire island. Moreover, he established a native clergy and provided for the continued goverance of the Church. By the time St. Patrick died in 461, Ireland was Christian.

The conversion of Ireland was important. It was the

first time that a land outside the Roman Empire had been wholly converted. Moreover, a very rigorous type of Catholicism and monasticism arose in Ireland. From the Irish monasteries were to come many missionaries to aid in the conversion of Europe.

The Arian Kingdoms. After the barbarian invasions three great areas of the Roman Empire were under the control of Arian Christians: Italy, North Africa, and Spain. Naturally the Church wished these lands to return to the true Faith. Success, however, was not to be as pronounced as with the pagan barbarians.

In Italy the Ostrogoths held away. Theodoric, their leader, did not persecute the Church but his people remained Arian. Ostrogothic power was soon extinguished, however. In 535 Justinian, an Eastern emperor determined to reconquer the West, landed an army in Italy and soon re-established control. At best, this was a mixed blessing for the Church, because Justinian and his successors constantly intervened in spiritual affairs, much to the detriment of the papacy. In some ways the rule of the tolerant heretic, Theodoric, had been better.

In North Africa the story was even more discouraging. There the Vandals carried out a brutal persecution which practically annihilated the true Christians. The Vandals were never really converted. Justinian restored Roman control over the area for a short time, but then the rapid rise of Mohammedanism swept all before it and North Africa was lost to the Faith.

Only in Visigothic Spain was full success achieved. There the king, Leovigild, began a persecution in 584. But already Catholicism was making progress and among the converts was Hermenegild, one of the king's sons, who was put to death for his Faith. Leovigild soon regretted his action, however, and his successor, Recared, went even further. Recared became king in 589 and impressed by the courage of his brother, Hermenegild, he gave up his Arian beliefs, and along with a great number of his warriors accepted conversion to the true Faith. Spain thus became Catholic.

The Franks. Already, however, the Church had achieved a far more important victory: the conversion of the Franks. At the end of the fifth century they were ruled by an energetic young leader named Clovis. Clovis was himself a pagan but his wife, Clotilda, was a devoted Christian and her good example soon led to results. In the heat of a great battle against the Alemanni, Clovis called upon the Christian God to save him from defeat. Clovis won the battle and, as a result, he and a great number of his followers accepted baptism from St. Remigius in the year 496.

Baptism, of course, did not completely Christianize the Franks. Clovis' personal life continued to be a scandal, and murder, especially for political reasons, remained all too common. Furthermore, the attempt of the Frankish king to spread the Faith by the use of the sword displayed a serious misunderstanding of the nature of Christianity. Further, Clovis and his successors ruled the Church with an iron hand, and many unworthy bishops and abbots were appointed due to their influence. But these failings would eventually be overcome and they did not detract from the fact that France, "the eldest daughter of the Church," had become Catholic.

England. Christianity had long existed in England, since during the period of Roman rule the native Britons had accepted the Faith. During the barbarian invasions, however, the island was overrun by Angles, Saxons, and Jutes, all of whom were pagans. Unfortunately, the native Britons, out of hatred and fear for the invaders, did nothing to convert them. Even missionaries from the Irish monasteries were unable to achieve any significant success. Another and greater effort was to be required for the conversion of England. This effort resulted from the work of the papacy.

From 590 to 604 St. Gregory the Great ruled as pope. A highly educated and cultured man, he was destined to be one of the greatest popes in the history of the Church. A spiritual writer of unusual ability and an advocate of Church music, he was also most active in his encouragement of Benedictine monasticism. He was also greatly interested in the missionary activity of the Church.

Thus, in 596 Pope Gregory sent St. Augustine of Canterbury and some 40 monks to England. The mission was extremely successful. Augustine won the favor of many of the native kings and the Faith spread rapidly, despite Briton hostility to the missionaries. By 601 St. Augustine was consecrated "Bishop of England." After his death the work continued and it was not long until all England embraced Christianity. Moreover, the English Church was an especially vigorous one. The work of St. Bede (672-735), whose *Ecclesiastical History of the English People* is of great historical value, demonstrated the remarkable brilliance of Catholic intellectual life in England.

Germany. The conversion of Germany was an equally important development. There had been several early attempts to convert the area. Frankish bishops were responsible for some missions, and Irish monks also made significant efforts. But in a real sense the conversion of Germany awaited the conversion of England, since the English were to be instrumental in winning Germany for the Church. The English Benedictines possessed an organizational genius that was difficult to equal and they soon put it to good use in the service of Christ.

The first great victory within the German lands was the conversion of the Frisians who lived in what is today Holland. This was the work of St. Willibrord and several

English monks. By 695 St. Willibrord had achieved so much success that he was consecrated "Bishop of the Frisians." An important base for the conversion of all Germany was thus established.

Another Englishman, Wynfrith, completed the missionary work in Germany in the first half of the eighth century. Wynfrith, known to us as St. Boniface (680-753), went to Rome in 719 to get the approval of the pope to carry the Faith into Germany. This was quickly granted and in 722 Boniface was consecrated "Bishop of Germany." Aided by a great number of English monks the work went steadily forward. Churches and monasteries were established and the converts were trained in their Faith. By 732 progress was so great that St. Boniface was made an archbishop with the power to consecrate other bishops. Boniface himself was martyred in 753 but by that time the greater part of Germany had become Christian.

Other Missions. With the conversion of Germany all of Western and Central Europe had been won for the Faith. Missionary activity did not, however, cease. There was also an attempt to convert Scandinavia. In the ninth century St. Ansgar, a Frankish monk, carried Christianity into Denmark and baptized its king in 826. Beyond this, however, little progress was made, for the people of Norway and Sweden did not accept the Faith until near the end of the tenth century. The delay was fatal, for the Vikings or Northmen of Scandinavia were to inflict much suffering on Western Europe in a long series of invasions.

More success was achieved among the Slavic people in Eastern Europe. Here the work of two brothers, Saints Cyril and Methodius, was decisive. Having received permission from the pope to use the Slavic language in the liturgy, they enjoyed much success. Throughout the ninth and tenth centuries the conversion of Bulgaria, Russia,

Hungary, and Poland followed. But the Slavic Church was to suffer serious problems. Quarrels between the pope and the bishop of Constantinople were frequent with regard to the Slavs, and when the break between the Eastern and Western Churches occurred, only Poland and Hungary remained loyal to Rome.

Summary. By the end of the tenth century, then, Christianity had established itself throughout Europe, but there was still much to be done. In every area there remained pockets of pagans still to be reached. Moreover, it was one thing to baptize a barbarian; it was something else to fully Christianize him. Old superstitions and pagan morality were hard to overcome. Thus, there were many difficulties and abuses.

The above considerations do not, however, efface the fact that the barbarians had been converted. Some of the factors which made possible so notable an achievement should be briefly noted. The grace of God and the guiding hand of the Holy Spirit were, of course, of prime importance. Christian devotion to a spirit of charity was also of significance. It required, for example, a great amount of true Christian love for St. Patrick to return to the land of his captors in order to convert them. In many places, too, the good example of one individual had a significant effect in winning their country to the Faith. In Spain it was the courage of Hermenegild, in France it was the quiet patience of Clotilda. Also, the zeal and ability of the missionaries must be noted. The fact that they placed so much effort on converting and winning the favor of native chieftains reveals their striking knowledge of the barbarian personality. Finally, the encouragement and guidance provided by the papacy made possible and properly organized the work of the missionaries. Without such organization, so vast a task as the conversion of an entire continent would not have been possible.

The Founding of the Papal State

While the conversion of the West was proceeding, important events were occurring in Italy. Since Constantine's toleration of Christianity, the Church had acquired a great deal of property, primarily as the result of gifts from the faithful. As a result, the Church soon became one of the largest landowners in all of Italy. The pope, of course, controlled this property and quite naturally he became increasingly important as a temporal ruler. With the coming of the barbarians the prestige and power of the papacy increased still more. In the absence of any other authority, the pope became the real ruler of Rome and its surrounding countryside. Necessarily, then, the pope became embroiled in a great number of complex political problems.

The Situation in Italy. With the fall of the Roman Empire Italy became a place of disorder. The coming of the Ostrogoths presented the Church with the threat of a regime that was frankly heretical in its religion. This threat was removed when the armies of Justinian reconquered the peninsula, but the power of the emperor at Constantinople was never strong in Italy. Constantinople had too many enemies of its own to govern effectively an area so far away. Moreover, the Eastern emperors displayed a distressing tendency to intervene in spiritual questions and more than once used violence against the papacy. Quite naturally, the pope felt insecure.

The Lombards. The anxiety of the pope was increased when, in 568, a new barbarian tribe, the Lombards, made their way into Italy. Under a long line of capable leaders, the Lombards began to attack the power of the emperor in Italy and even to threaten Rome itself. The popes were thus put in a serious position. They wished to remain loyal to the emperor and, indeed, feared to break with him because of the already strained religious relations between East and West. At the same time they feared the Lombards and realized that the emperor either would not or could not protect them. The need for a new protector was clear. But to whom could the papacy turn?

The Franks. To the north of Italy lay the kingdom of the Franks, a powerful people who since the conversion of Clovis had been Catholic. An unusual political situation within the Frankish kingdom provided the popes with an opportunity to secure them as allies. Since the death of Clovis the Merovingians, his successors, had ruled the country. But they were very weak kings, the "do-nothing" Merovingians they were called. The real power was exercised by the Mayors of the Palace. In 751 Pepin the Short, who was Mayor of the Palace and anxious to become king, sent a mission to Pope St. Zachary (741-752). Who should be king, asked Pepin? He who has legal title to the throne or he who actually has the power to rule? The pope decided that the man who actually rules should be king and, as a result, Pepin deposed the last Merovingian and had himself crowned and anointed king of the Franks by St. Boniface. In effect, the papacy had found its protector.

The Establishment of the Papal State. Very shortly the protector was needed. Aistulf, the king of the Lombards, began another attempt to conquer Rome. Finding help nowhere else, Pope Stephen II (752-757) appealed to Pepin and in 754 went to Frankland to confer with him. An alliance was quickly arranged and Pepin showed himself a willing subject of the papacy. Twice he invaded Italy to defeat the Lombards and save Rome. Then, in a document known as the Donation of Pepin, he granted the pope authority over Rome and a large part of central Italy. The pope had become a temporal ruler. The step was important for it guaranteed the pope a certain independence of action and freed him from his dependence on the Eastern emperor. Until 1870 the pope was to continue as a temporal ruler of the city of Rome.

The Carolingian Empire

The cooperation between the papacy and the Franks, which resulted in the erection of the Papal State, also manifested itself in other ways. The Franks had restored the power of the papacy. Might not they also be able to revive imperial power in all of Western Europe? Ever since the fall of Rome men had continued to believe in the necessity and advantages of a European Empire. Indeed, the possibility of cooperation between the Church and a restored Christian empire was a glittering one, difficult to resist. The attempt to achieve it was soon made.

Charlemagne. In the year 768 Pepin died and his son, Charlemagne (Charles the Great), became king of the Franks. Only twenty-six years old, he was an extremely capable ruler and perhaps the greatest general since Julius Caesar. Very quickly he consolidated his rule over Frankland and began to extend his power until nearly all of Western and Central Europe owed allegiance to him in some way or other. Moreover, Charlemagne was a more effective ruler than the barbarian world had previously seen. By sending out representatives known as *Missi Dominici*, he kept in close touch with all his realm. Moreover, he issued a great number of *capillaries*, or laws, to govern his kingdom. A man with the power of Charlemagne was important for the Church.

Charlemagne and the Church. Fortunately, Charlemagne was a sincere and devoted Christian, despite certain failings in his personal life. His love of the Faith was displayed in the great cathedral which he built at Aachen, his capital. Moreover, he rendered a great service to the papacy. The Lombards had again grown powerful and were threatening Rome. Thus in 774 he took his army into Italy and defeated Desiderius, the Lombard king. To prevent further trouble Charlemagne made himself king of the Lombards and confirmed the pope as the rightful ruler of Rome. Naturally, the papacy looked with favor on such a man.

The Revival of the Empire. In the year 800 while Charlemagne attended Christmas Mass in Rome, Pope Leo III set a crown upon his head and the Roman populace cried out, "Long life and victory to Charlemagne, the great and pacific emperor of the Romans, crowned of God." Seemingly, the Empire once more existed and Church-State cooperation was apparently assured.

The reality, however, did not always match the dream. To be sure, Charlemagne did a great deal for the Faith. His laws sought to maintain high standards in the clergy, and he was a determined enemy of heresy. At the same time, he promoted a remarkable revival of learning and culture. His Palace School, presided over by the English monk Alcuin, attracted the best scholars in Europe. But there were also failings. His attempt to convert the Saxons by force displayed a misunderstanding of true Christian doctrine. Moreover, the balance between spiritual and political power was difficult to maintain. Charlemagne tended to consider himself the ruler of the Church and thus he was prone to intervene in purely religious questions. As long as it was Charlemagne who interfered, however, it was not so bad, for he was truly devoted to the welfare of the Church. When the same approach was later used by less scrupulous rulers, serious abuses resulted.

Decline of the Empire. Charlemagne's Empire, however, was essentially weak. In reality, it was a ship of civilization in a barbarian sea and it soon sprang leaks.

A Charlemagne was required to keep it afloat and men of such stature are not common. His successor, Louis the Pious (814-840), was well-intentioned, but weak. Then a combination of unfortunate events—squabbles between Louis and his sons, the decay of imperial institutions, and the coming of new barbarians—brought about the collapse of the Empire. The dream had lasted only a short time. It was followed by the nightmare of a new "dark age" in which the Church, as well as society, found itself in deadly peril.

Feudalism and the Decline of the Church

The Dissolution of Society. During the ninth and tenth centuries Europe was visited by a series of new invasions. From the South came the forces of *Islam,* the followers of Mohammed, intent on spreading their religion to all Europe. By the ninth century, they controlled the Mediterranean Sea, most of Spain, and constantly threatened other areas. From the East came the *Magyars,* a new barbarian tribe sweeping out of Asia. But worst of all, there were the *Northmen* or *Vikings* who swept down out of Scandinavia to pillage and plunder all of Western Europe. No area that could be reached by water was safe from their violence. To make matters worse, there was no authority to oppose these invaders, for after the death of Louis the Pious the Carolingian Empire existed in name only. As a result, society quickly disintegrated.

Feudalism. In the midst of the invasions life became insecure and men fell back on local resources for protection. If the imperial government could do nothing, perhaps the local nobleman could. Thus arose the system known as feudalism. Men gave up their land and bound themselves to the nobility who, in turn, agreed to protect them and carry on the functions of government. Soon a complex system of personal relationships emerged. Ordinary peasants were bound to local noblemen, these noblemen in turn placed themselves under still stronger nobles, and so on. Society thus dissolved into a graduated system in which each rank had corresponding rights and duties.

Feudalism and the Church. In many ways feudalism met the needs of the time. It was, however, inevitable that the Church would be caught up in the feudal system, and this led to serious abuses.

The monasteries were very quickly involved. Because of the need for protection most of them placed themselves under the patronage of a nobleman. They thus became the nobleman's property and he usually reserved the right to appoint or, at least unduly influence the election of the abbot. The result was a general decay of monastic life. Many abbots appointed by the nobles were interested only in the income from the monasteries, and the monks were often left to their own devices. Under such conditions it is not surprising that immorality grew up and that, under unworthy abbots, true monastic ideals were forgotten.

Even more serious was the decline that affected the bishops. In these years bishops were frequently important civic and political officials. Quite naturally, then, kings and noblemen were interested in having bishops favorable to themselves. Charlemagne, for example, had appointed the bishops in Frankland. This custom persisted and as feudalism grew, most bishops were appointed and even invested with their office by kings and nobles, in spite of the fact that Church Law specifically stated that bishops were to be elected by the clergy of the cathedral. The result was that many bishops emphasized their political functions over their religious duties. Even worse was the fact that many unworthy men, having influence with the king, secured the position of bishop in order to gain control of the wealth which the Church possessed. Quite naturally the churches and the faithful were frequently neglected.

Even ordinary parish priests were affected. At this time

most parishes were founded and built by laymen, usually nobles. The local noble, for example, usually maintained a church for himself and his peasants. The noble also usually reserved to himself the right to appoint the parish priest, who was then ordained by the bishop. The results were predictable. Many unworthy men were appointed. Even more common, however, was the lack of proper education for those who became priests.

The Papacy. The whole trend of the time, then, was toward a serious "lay domination" of the Church. Even the papacy did not escape the general decline. The last strong pope was Nicholas I (858-867), a man who understood the responsibilities of his office and stood up for his rights. After his death decay set in. The pope, of course, was the ruler of Rome. Thus the office of the papacy was a political plum well worth the picking, and powerful Roman families soon began quarreling over the office. The result was that nine of the forty-four popes who reigned between 867 and 1048 met violent deaths. Even worse was the fact that a few of the popes were immoral men.

The lowest point of all was reached during the reign of John XII (955-964), a man who pursued pleasure to the detriment of everything else. Moreover, John's political dealings won him a great many enemies and, as a result, he took a step that was to seriously effect the position of the papacy. Needing a protector, John called the German king, Otto I, into Italy and proceeded to crown him Holy Roman Emperor. In reality John had found a master rather than a protector for Otto secured from him the promise that in the future no pope could be elected without the consent of the emperor. The result was turmoil. The Roman citizens were not happy with the arrangement and time and time again Otto and his successors had to intervene violently in Rome to maintain their man on the papal throne.

As the year 1000 approached many Christians were

fearful that the world was about to end. To the often superstitious European of the time, 1000 seemed a nice round number with which to consummate the history of the world. Moreover, the general decline of the Church seemed to betoken some great calamity. The world, however, did not end nor did the Church remain in her abject condition. Christ had promised to remain with His Church until the end of time and the promise was soon to bear fruit.

The Medieval Reformation

Despite the poor condition of the Church during these centuries, there were always some men of upright lives anxious to carry out reform. Moreover, the guidance of the Holy Spirit was slowly preparing the way for a rebirth.

The Cluniac Reform. The first great reform movement came from the monasteries. In the year 910, an abbot named Berno founded the monastery of Cluny in France under the protection of Duke William of Aquitaine. From the beginning it was unique. Cluny was free from all lay authority and was governed solely by an abbot freely elected by the monks. The result was that, under a long line of saintly abbots, the rule of St. Benedict was restored and all abuses were avoided. Soon other monasteries placed themselves under the direction of the abbot of Cluny until a whole network of reformed monasteries existed. A general improvement in monastic life resulted and from these monasteries the spirit of reform quickly spread.

Objectives of the Reformers. As the movement for reform matured, those leading it began to single out especially serious abuses on which to concentrate their attack. There were three which seemed to call for immediate attention. The first of these was *simony*—that is, the

46

selling of a spiritual office. Quite often during these centuries bishoprics were literally bought and sold. A man wishing the office was forced to pay a sum of money to the king or nobleman who had the power of appointment. The abuse became even more serious when the bishop, having secured the position, attempted to make up his losses by selling the office of the priesthood or by overtaxing the parishes.

A second abuse was *clerical marriage.* According to Church law, priests in the West were forbidden to marry. The law, however, was commonly ignored and these rare bishops who tried to enforce it were often opposed with violence. Thus, priests, bishops, and even monks married, or what is worse, lived openly in sin with concubines. Spiritual offices were often passed down from father to son by heredity. While much of this can be attributed to ignorance rather than immorality, the cause for scandal was nonetheless great.

The third abuse was *lay investiture*—that is, the custom of a king or nobleman appointing a bishop or abbot and then conferring on him the insignia of his spiritual office: the ring and crozier. The abuse arose from the system of feudalism and from the medieval confusion of things political and spiritual. It was, however, the most serious of the abuses since it was the indirect cause of the other two. The fact that laymen appointed ecclesiastical officials meant that many unworthy men were appointed—men without a true religious vocation—and it was precisely such men as these who were most inclined to be guilty of simony and clerical marriage. Lay investiture, then, lay at the root of the problem.

The Reform of the Papacy. Attempts at reform were many and much good was accomplished. The reformed monasteries spread their influence to much advantage. Certain kings, such as Alfred the Great of England (871-899) also carried out worthwhile reforms. But no lasting improvement was possible until the papacy itself had been reformed. The change came with the election of Pope St. Leo IX (1049-1054). He restored dignity to the office, encouraged reform, and gathered about him capable men interested in improving the state of the Church. His successors carried on in this tradition. Pope Nicholas II (1059-1061) ruled that only the College of Cardinals should have any voice in the election of the pope. This was a particularly important step for it began the process of freeing the papacy from the power of the Roman nobles and the German emperors.

Gregory VII and Henry IV.   Among the most prominent of the reformers around the papacy was the monk Hildebrand. In 1073 he was elected pope and took the name of Gregory VII. Determined to reform the Church, he realized that lay investiture would have to be opposed vigorously. An enemy soon appeared, the German Emperor Henry IV. Henry, an exceptionally violent and stubborn man, placed much importance on his power to control ecclesiastical appointments. Gregory, too, was noted for his iron determination and the stage was thus set for an epic struggle. In 1075 Henry forced out of office the legitimate bishop of the city of Milan and installed his own candidates. A long war of words followed and in 1076, Gregory excommunicated Henry. Circumstances helped him because the German nobles used the excommunication as a pretext for rebellion against the emperor. Henry was left defenseless, so he journeyed to Italy, stood three days barefooted in the snow before Canossa, and begged the pope's forgiveness. Finally Gregory gave way, forgave the emperor of his sins, and lifted the ban of excommunication. Gregory had won the first round.

Henry, however, soon showed that he had no intention of reforming his ways. Having regained his power, he continued to invest bishops and to oppose the pope.

Consequently, Gregory once again excommunicated him in 1080. This time, however, Henry marched on the city of Rome with an army, captured it, and drove Gregory into exile. Seemingly in disgrace, the pope died in 1085. Gregory's efforts had not been in vain, however, for he had effectively challenged the imperial domination of the Church. The tide was about to turn.

The Concordat of Worms. After the deaths of Gregory VII and Henry IV the struggle between Church and empire continued. By 1122, however, both sides were growing weary and the opportunity for a settlement was at hand. The result was the Concordat of Worms signed by the Emperor Henry V and Pope Callixtus II. It provided that bishops were henceforth to be elected by the clergy of the cathedral. The emperor was allowed to be present at such elections but violence or threats were forbidden. Moreover, the emperor was forbidden to invest ecclesiastical officials with the spiritual insignia of their office, although he still might confer the political insignia.

The concordat was therefore a compromise. Opportunity for an unscrupulous emperor to influence elections still existed. Nonetheless, the Church had won a significant victory. The distinction between spiritual and political power was recognized and the Church's control over the former was acknowledged. As a result, the reform movement went steadily forward. Abuses such as simony and clerical marriage soon became rare, and the Church was restored to a healthy condition.

The Eastern Schism

The Church had resisted the lay domination of feudalism and had overcome the confusion resulting from the second wave of barbarian invasions. One fact, however, marred the victory: the schism which split the Eastern Church from the papacy and which still persists today.

Causes of the Schism. Many factors served to cut the East off from the West. First, the Roman Empire in the East had never fallen and, as a result, the Eastern emperor exercised a rigid control over the Church. Nor were relations between emperor and pope cordial. Eastern emperors frequently intervened in purely spiritual questions, and more. than once they attempted to use violence against the pope to enforce their views. Relations were not improved when the papacy recognized Charlemagne as emperor in the West and appealed to him to act as its protector in Italy not only against the Lombards but also the Eastern Emperor.

Secondly, there were cultural differences between East and West. The urbane Greeks tended to consider those in the West as uncultured barbarians and this, in turn, weakened their loyalty to the papacy. Thirdly, there were differences of religious practice. The Eastern Church, for example, used Greek in the Mass and permitted their priests to marry. Finally, there were endless points of controversy and dispute between the two Churches, and these must be briefly examined.

Iconoclasm. During the eighth century a serious dispute arose. The Emperor Leo III (717-740) decided for unknown reasons that the use of art in the churches and the veneration of the saints were sinful practices. Thus he embarked on a policy of iconoclasm—that is, the destruction of sacred images. Many opposed this policy, and St. John of Damascus presented the true Catholic teaching: the veneration of sacred pictures is permissible and even to be encouraged unless, of course, there is an actual worship of them. But Leo maintained his policy.

In 753 Emperor Constantine V convened a council of Eastern bishops. The council, thoroughly intimidated by the emperor, declared that the veneration of sacred images was an heretical practice. A persecution followed and a break with the papacy seemed imminent. But Irene, the wife of Emperor Leo IV, brought about a reconciliation. Another council of Eastern bishops was convened at Nicaea in 787. It reversed the previous council, declaring that the veneration of images was consistent with Catholic doctrine and that iconoclasm was a heresy. The breach was thus healed, but bad feelings and distrust remained.

The Photian Schism. In the ninth century another crisis occurred. It involved a dispute as to who was the legitimate Patriarch of Constantinople. Emperor Bardas forced out of office the rightful patriarch and appointed in his place a certain Photius. When the pope refused to accept the change, the emperor convened an Eastern council which proceeded to declare the pope excommunicated. Once again, however, the breach was healed. But another cause for dispute was arising. The Slavic lands—Bulgaria, Poland, Hungary, and Russia—were then being converted and a bitter contest developed over the control of the area.

The Final Break came during the years 1043 to 1059. It was the work of Michael Cerularius, the Patriarch of Constantinople. For reasons which are still not clear he precipitated a split. Cerularius insisted that certain Western practices were heretical: the use of unleavened bread and the insistence on clerical celibacy, for example. A full break then occurred and since that time the Eastern Church has refused to acknowledge the authority of the papacy. The first great split in the ranks of Christianity had taken place.

Christian Life in the Early Middle Ages

Christian life and practices were greatly effected by the coming of the barbarians. As a group they were often rude, vulgar, and subject to much superstition. Nor did baptism immediately remove these blemishes. Centuries were required for the work of civilizing and fully Christianizing these new converts. The Church, however, showed itself sympathetic. While it condemned the worst abuses it nonetheless patiently and slowly sought to re-form barbarian misunderstandings. The Church also succeeded in softening the hardness and cruelty of barbarian life and customs. And in the midst of a barbarian sea, the Church—and especially the monasteries—preserved the essentials of Western culture.

Christian life was also greatly affected by the remarkable growth of the Church in these centuries. Previously, Christians had been only a small minority of the population. Men willing to suffer persecution for their faith were, of course, rigorous in the observance of morality. When the Church expanded, however, so that most of the population of Europe was Christian, the same dedication was not to be expected. But this change should not be seen purely as a weakness. Christ intended His Church for all men, not just a select, dedicated few. Moreover, as Christ showed Himself sympathetic to human weakness, the Church could do no less. Thus, while much of the former severity disappeared, the Church was serving and bringing salvation to a much greater number of men.

Church Organization. As has been seen, the hierarchy of the Church underwent many difficulties during these centuries. Yet, the picture is by no means all black. The papacy, despite a few bad popes, remained, as Christ had intended, the head of the Church. Moreover, the popes maintained the doctrinal integrity of the Faith. No pope, irrespective of his personal life, ever attempted to teach or spread an heretical doctrine. Nor should it be forgotten that it was the papacy that eventually led and won the movement for reform. The position of the bishops also remained secure despite the existence of abuses. Not all bishops used the wealth at their disposal for personal gain. Instead, many used it for charitable and educational purposes and devoted themselves to the reform of the Church.

On the lower levels of the clergy important advances

were also made. During the early part of the Middle Ages the Church faced an important organizational problem. Now that so many converts were being won the need for churches was growing. Should each church and each small city have its own bishop? The Church very soon decided in the negative. Instead, the parish system was developed. Rural areas and small towns were to have their spiritual needs taken care of by priests, subject to a bishop in a nearby large city.

There were, of course, abuses among the ranks of these lower clergy. But the great weakness was ignorance, not immorality, and already steps were being taken to provide a better and fuller education for the clergy, under the auspices of the bishop. At the same time, a distinctive clerical dress was being developed and the law of the Church forbidding clerical marriage, while difficult in the beginning to enforce, was a step in the right direction.

Popular Religion. It showed many interesting developments during these centuries. Many customs were introduced which have remained until the present day. The veneration of saints and of their relics was a very common religious practice and the making of pilgrimages was a very popular means of religious devotion. It is true, also, that there was a mixture of superstition in many religious practices of the day, but it is important to note that people of the early Middle Ages at least recognized that religion was an essential part of everyday life, rather than something merely reserved for special days.

The Liturgy. During the early Middle Ages there was a standardization of the liturgy. Previously there had been a great number of local variations in the form of the Mass and other religious ceremonies. These were gradually eliminated and the Western Church began to follow the usage of Rome, especially with regard to the Mass. The liturgical year was also more fully defined. Prominent feasts such as Easter and Pentecost were observed everywhere at the same time. Christmas, feasts in honor of Mary, and All Saints Day were also celebrated. Finally, the beginning of the observance of Lent is to be found in these years.

The Sacraments. The baptism of infants became the accepted practice during these centuries. Previously, many Christians had put off baptism until late in life. Usually confirmation was administered at the same time as baptism, and even in the case of infants Holy Communion was given.

Reception of Communion was frequent during these centuries, although there were changes in the method of administering the sacrament. In the beginning the faithful received both wine and bread. Often the wine was taken through a straw and later the custom grew up of dipping the bread in the wine. Slowly, however, there was an evolution in the direction of administering Communion in the form of the bread alone, a change that was necessary in order to prevent any contamination of the Sacred Blood in the process of administering the sacrament.

Confession, too, underwent changes. Everywhere the sacrament was now given in private. Moreover, the penance which had once been public was more and more taking the form of private prayers. Finally, confession was viewed more as a means of gaining grace, rather than simply a means of having serious sins forgiven, and thus the sacrament was received more frequently.

Conclusion

The early Middle Ages were difficult times for the Church. Yet the Church overcame its adversities. It withstood the barbarian invasions and converted the continent of Europe, for the missionary spirit was by no means dead. It also withstood the system of feudalism with all its abuses, and eventually it reformed them. In these difficult centuries the Church continued to be the rock of Faith and of culture as well. Indeed, the story of the Church in the early Middle Ages is a significant proof of the power of God to sustain His work. It is also an eloquent testimony to those who, however weak, cooperated with His grace for the benefit of their souls and those of all mankind. By the end of the eleventh century the Church stood ready to carry on the work of salvation and civilization with renewed vigor.

STUDY QUESTIONS

1. How did the monks of the early Middle Ages show that they understood the missionary nature of the Christian message?
2. What events of this period of Church History made it difficult for the Church to carry out her primary purpose in the world?
3. What events of this age show that the people of God cannot rest from the work of reforming themselves and the institutions they set up to carry out the two-fold commandment of charity?
4. What problems do the followers of Christ face when they live in a completely Christian community that they do not face when they are a small minority in a pagan world?
5. For the Christian of today to carry out the work of the re-union of the Christian community, what must he remember of the history of the Church in the early Middle Ages?
6. In what way does this time in the history of the Christian community suggest that it is not possible for the Church to live apart from the world and its history?

Bibliography

BIELER, L. *The Life and Legend of St. Patrick.* (Dublin: 1949).
(A good biography.)

CONCANNON, HELENA. *St. Patrick.* (London: 1931).
(A competent biography.)

DEWOHL, LOUIS. *Citadel of God, A Novel of St. Benedict.* (Philadelphia: 1959).
(A popular account of the greatest figure in Western monasticism.)

GREENAWAY, G. W. *St. Boniface.* (London: 1955).
(A good biography of the most important figure in the conversion of Germany.)

HOWORTH, HENRY H. *Saint Gregory the Great.* (London: 1912).
(A good biography of one of the greatest of all the popes.)

NUGENT, DON PETER. *St. Benedict.* (London: 1924).
(A good popular biography.)

STEPHENS, W. R. *Hildebrand and His Times.* (London: 1914).
(A good biography of Pope St. Gregory VII.)

Chapter III

The Church in the Later Middle Ages

CHRIST SHEPHERDS HIS PEOPLE

Introduction

THE reform movement so vigorously encouraged by Pope St. Gregory VII and his successors had ended many of the worst abuses in the Church. Moreover, it had put the papacy in a position to effectively oppose the threats of the German emperors. In addition, Europe was entering a new age: the turmoil of earlier centuries gave way to a new stability. For the first time the Church was able to live in a world which it had largely created. The next two centuries—the twelfth and thirteenth— were an age in which all Europe was organized around the Christian Faith. So great was the power and prestige of the Church that many have called this period an "Age of Faith." If the position of the Church was occasionally challenged in these years, it still remains true that its power was the great reality of the age.

The Conflict between Empire and Papacy

The Issue. The problem of the relation between Church and state is an old one and the Church has seldom, if ever, been free from it. The problem grew particularly severe, however, in the later Middle Ages. The conflict of Gregory VII and Henvy IV over lay investiture was only an opening gun in the battle. Before Gregory VII the German emperors had often dominated the Church, controlling ecclesiastical appointments and deposing and setting up popes as their power allowed. Gregory had opposed this lay domination and the Concordat of Worms confirmed his victory. But the struggle did not end. Behind the question of lay investiture was an even more serious one: Who was supreme? Pope or emperor? Church or state?

The Papal View. Pope Gregory VII did not wish the Church to dominate the state; he only wanted the Church to be free from the state so that it could properly exercise its spiritual functions. But the success of Gregory VII and his successors led others to the position that the Church was indeed superior to the state, just as the soul is superior to the body. As long as it was applied to spiritual questions this was a valid argument. The attempt to apply it to purely political questions was another matter. Yet some defenders of the papacy insisted that the pope was the ultimate political authority in Europe. He therefore had the power not only to excommunicate an emperor, they said, but to depose him as well.

Opponents of the papal view, however, rejected this argument. They held that the power of the emperor came directly from God and was independent of the pope. Thus, the pope might legitimately excommunicate the emperor since this was a spiritual matter, but he could not depose him because that was purely a political question. The emperors, however, were not content with mere independence from the papacy. They were determined to restore the old Roman Empire. To do so, however, required them to subjugate Italy. As a result, the position of the papacy was threatened since the pope was the ruler of Rome and Central Italy. If the emperor succeeded in controlling this area he would, in fact, reduce the pope to a mere subject of the Empire.

In the Middle Ages, then, there seemed no possibility of compromise. Either pope or emperor would dominate, and the Church could ill afford another era of lay control.

Troubles in Rome. After the Concordat of Worms in 1122 the papacy was confronted with an ugly situation in the city of Rome. Conflicts among powerful Roman families seeking to control the papacy did not come to an end. When Pope Honorius II died in 1130 difficulty followed. The College of Cardinals split and the different factions each elected their own pope. Innocent II, the legitimately elected pontiff, was driven from Rome and Anacletus II, the pretender, took possession of the city. For eight years the struggle continued while each man attempted to gain recognition as true pope. Finally, in 1138 Anacletus died and Innocent II was universally recognized. But Rome was still restive and in 1143 a revolt broke out. Innocent was driven from the city and a republic was established. Led by Arnold of Brescia, a cleric who denounced the political power of the Church, the republic lasted for over ten years. It was not until the reign of Pope Adrian IV (1154-59), the only English pope, that papal government was restored to Rome.

Frederick Barbarossa, emperor of Germany, then reopened the old struggle with the papacy. At first friendly with Pope Adrian, Frederick was nonetheless determined to bring Italy under his control. In 1158 the emperor invaded Northern Italy and imposed his will on the Lombard cities in that area. At this point Adrian died and the cardinals elected Alexander III (1159-81), a bitter enemy of the emperor, as pope. Many disagreements followed. Finally, in 1167, Frederick conquered the city of Rome, drove out the pope, and installed his own candidate. Only a plague, which many interpreted as a sign from heaven, forced the emperor to leave the city. In 1176 Frederick once more marched into Italy, but here he met defeat. At the battle of Legnano the cities of Northern Italy, allied with the pope, won a crushing victory. At the Peace of Constance, Frederick was forced to admit the liberty of Northern Italy and to accept Innocent III as the true pope. Once again, the papacy had won.

Trouble in England also bothered Pope Alexander III. The English king, Henry II, became involved in a bitter quarrel with Thomas à Becket, the archbishop of Canterbury. Finally, Becket was murdered by four of the king's knights in the cathedral. Popular opinion immediately condemned Henry, who was forced to do penance and made concessions to Pope Alexander III.

Henry VI, the son of Frederick Barbarossa, next tried to restore the power of the Empire. Due to a fortunate marriage, he became the king of Southern Italy and Sicily. Moreover, he refused to pay homage to the pope as the former rulers of the area had done. This was indeed dangerous because German control of Southern Italy meant that Rome was surrounded. The five popes who followed Alexander III, however, did nothing and only the death of Henry at the early age of thirty-two saved the papacy from great difficulty.

Pope Innocent III (1198-1216) then took the situation in hand. He has often been called the greatest of the medieval popes, since during his reign the political power of the papacy reached its greatest heights. While primarily interested in spiritual matters, Innocent did not hesitate to make use of thoroughly practical means to attain his ends. In at least three instances he fully demonstrated the power of the Church.

In Germany all was chaos after the death of Henry VI as rival factions contested for the throne. Despite the fact that hardly anyone in Germany admitted his right to do so, Innocent intervened in the struggle. It was probably a mistake, for his candidate, Otto of Brunswick, began to disregard the rights of the Church after he became emperor. Fortunately, however, Otto was soon defeated and Innocent then brought about the election of Frederick II, the king of Southern Italy, and the young son of Henry VI. This again was a mistake because Frederick, despite the fact that he had been brought up by Innocent, soon became the most determined foe the papacy had ever had.

In France, Innocent was more successful. When the king, Philip II, unlawfully divorced his first wife and married again, Innocent made use of every spiritual weapon at his disposal. As a result Philip II was finally forced to take back his first wife.

In England, the pope again proved victorious. There the incapable King John attempted to interfere in the election of the archbishop of Canterbury. When John refused to accept the pope's candidate, Innocent excommunicated him. Immediately a revolt broke out against the king who was forced to submit to the pope.

The Final Round. Despite the power of Innocent III the old conflict with the empire broke out again after his death. The new emperor, Frederick II, was a ruthless and cynical young man. Called "The Wonder of the World" by his contemporaries, he was determined to subject the Church to the state. Moreover, as both king of Southern Italy and emperor of Germany, he had the papacy in a vice. Pope Honorius III (1216-27) did nothing to provoke a struggle but trouble followed his death.

Frederick had promised to go on a crusade but time and time again he refused to do so. Finally, Pope Gregory IX (1227-41) excommunicated him. A long war followed. Peace efforts were made, but Frederick was not the kind of man to live up to troublesome agreements.

Pope Innocent IV (1243-54) eventually took the decisive steps. He again excommunicated the emperor and declared him deposed. Frederick for his part declared war on the papacy, but he was never able to win it and he died defeated in 1250. The war continued against all of Frederick's heirs until they too were defeated and killed. Popes after Innocent IV merely cemented the work. The power of the empire was broken.

The Meaning of the Struggle. The papacy had emerged victorious over all its opponents and the freedom of the Church from imperial control was assured. Moreover, the papacy had become the dominant political power in Europe. But all this was not completely favorable. Many resented papal power and questioned the Church's use of political and military means. Even St. Louis IX, the holy king of France, refused to recognize the power of the pope to depose Frederick II. Quite possibly the papacy had gone too far. Its political power was soon to lead to further struggles which would endanger its spiritual power as well.

The Institutional Development of the Church

The Influence of the Papacy. The papacy was able to win so many victories partly because of its great spiritual powers. By *excommunication* the pope could deprive any guilty person from membership in the Church, a dreaded punishment in an age when religion was taken seriously. Even more powerful was the use of *interdict*. By this device the pope could forbid the dispensing of the sacraments in any state or area. This was most effective, for the people so deprived would then put great pressure on the ruler whose crimes had caused the punishment. The power of the pope within the Church also grew because many recognized that the papacy was the best defense against abuses. Consequently, many things which had formerly been handled by local churches were turned over to the pope. Most important was the fact that he began to take a much larger part in the selection of bishops.

Papal Government. The growth of papal power quite naturally made necessary a growth in the machinery of papal government. New agencies and numerous assistants were required to aid the pope in his work. Great use, of course, was made of the cardinals, all of whom resided in Rome. But the real government machinery was in the *Papal Curia,* a body much like the court of a king. It was divided into three major agencies. The *chancery* took care of all correspondence and paper work. The *camera* was responsible for financial matters, but due to increasing needs the pope's financial position was always shaky, despite the money flowing in from all over Europe. The *papal courts* were the judicial branch of the government and the amount of their work increased as more and more cases were appealed to Rome from lower ecclesiastical courts. Finally, the popes made use of *legates,* or papal ambassadors. Their function was to explain the directives of the pope and to make sure that these were carried out. In addition, they kept in constant touch with the rulers of the various countries.

The Bishops and Lower Clergy. Despite the growth of papal power the bishops remained very important since they were geographically closer to the people. Moreover, bishops were now more effective due to their freedom from lay investiture. In theory, they continued to be elected by the cathedral clergy, although the pope had the right to intervene in any election and often did so.

The position of the lower clergy was more improved by the reforms of Gregory VII. But the great difficulty remained; the lack of any really sound education for most priests.

Church councils continued to carry on important functions in the Church. Between 1122 and 1294 some six general councils met. Most of them were originally called to deal with some particular problem, but all of them did much to further the reform of the Church. The continued condemnation of such abuses as simony and clerical marriage was typical of their work. In addition, the requirement that every Catholic must receive the sacraments of Penance and Holy Communion each year during the Easter Season, was passed by a council at this time.

New Religious Orders. During the twelfth century there were important developments within monasticism. The earlier Cluniac reform had lost its impetus and many were anxious to return to an even more rigorous standard of monastic life. The *Carthusians* founded by St. Bruno, for example, lived a strict contemplative life. The monks lived in individual huts and met only for sacred services.

There was also an attempt to revive the monastic life for ordinary priests. The *Premonstratensians* founded by St. Norbert lived as monks but engaged in missionary and pastoral work.

The most popular order of the century, however, was the *Cistercians* founded in 1098 by St. Robert Molesme. This order attempted to return to the strict Benedictine rule and great emphasis was placed on manual labor. The popularity of the order was further increased by the work of St. Bernard of Clairvaux who dominated the last half of the twelfth century. A great theologian and mystic, he did much valuable work for the Church.

Monasticism during the thirteenth century was somewhat different. The new orders accepted the idea of serving God by serving man, rather than concentrating solely on personal sanctity.

The *Franciscans* were founded by St. Francis of Assisi (1182-1226), one of the most appealing figures of the age.

The son of a wealthy family, he led a carefree life as a youth, but then dedicated himself to God. A group of companions joined him and in 1209 his rule was approved by the pope. Placing great stress on a life of poverty, St. Francis desired his order to concentrate on serving the poor and the oppressed.

The *Dominicans* were founded by St. Dominic Gusman (1170-1221). Perceiving the growth of heresy and the evil lives of many people, St. Dominic saw the need for an order that would concentrate on leading souls back to God by preaching the gospel. Moreover, he was determined that his monks should be well educated so that they might better carry out their mission. Thus, the order put great stress on intellectual achievement.

These were the two great orders of the thirteenth century. Both engaged in preaching, works of charity, and missionary activity. Both had connected to them an order of nuns, a development which fit in well with the growth of religious orders for women at the time. Finally, both played a large part in the intellectual revival that was sweeping Europe.

The Crusades

Mohammedanism. At the beginning of the seventh century a new religion arose in Arabia. It was called *Mohammedanism* after its founder, Mohammed (570-632). Little is known of his early life, but as a young man he married a wealthy widow and led a luxurious life. At about the age of forty, however, he experienced what he believed to be a revelation from heaven. More "visions" followed and soon Mohammed had constructed a body of religious beliefs. His basic doctrines were recorded by his disciples in a book known as the *Koran.* A mixture of Judaism, Christianity, and Arabic religious ideas, the religion was simple. The follower had first of all to worship one god, Allah, and to acknowledge that Mohammed was his last and greatest prophet. He was also required to pray, give alms to the poor, fast for a certain period each year, and if possible, make a pilgrimage to Mecca, the holy city of the new religion. For those who were faithful, Mohammed promised a heaven of sensuous pleasures.

At first rejected in Arabia, the new religion soon made tremendous progress, partly because of Mohammed's teaching that all who died fighting against unbelievers were assured of heaven. Thus, by the time Mohammed died, most of Arabia had been converted, largely by force. By the end of the seventh century the entire Near East had been won, and in the early eighth century North Africa and Spain were conquered. The Mohammedans soon began to put great pressure on Europe and especially on the Byzantine Empire.

Origin of the Crusades. As early as the seventh century the Mohammedans controlled the city of Jerusalem. But for a long time they allowed Christians to make pilgrimages there. About the eleventh century, however, the Seljuk Turks came into the Near East, accepted the religion of Mohammed, and assumed control of the area. Fanatic Mohammedans, they began to persecute Christians and to stop pilgrimages to Jerusalem. They also threatened the Byzantine Empire which frantically appealed to the West for aid.

As soon as the Turks began their persecution the papacy was anxious to take action. Obviously, it desired to protect Christians and also to deliver the Holyland from the hands of unbelievers. But there were other motives. The possibility of a war against the Turks led by the popes was seen as a great opportunity to increase papal prestige. In addition, there was the hope that the challenge of such a struggle would serve to end the many petty wars then going on in Europe. Finally, there was the belief that a religious reunion with the Eastern Church could be achieved if the West would come to the

66

aid of Byzantium against the Turks. Thus on November 18, 1095, at Clermont, France, Pope Urban II announced a crusade against the Turks. The response of the crowd was a spontaneous cry: "God wills it." Other preachers spread the word, and everywhere enthusiasm was great. Many immediately volunteered. Almost all had a genuine religious desire to recapture the Holyland, but for some the desire for land, wealth, and adventure was also involved.

The Initial Victory. The *First Crusade* was led by nobles from France and Sicily. In separate groups they reached Constantinople in 1097 and then prepared to attack the Turks. A long and bitter campaign followed. Finally, in July of 1099 the crusaders captured the city of Jerusalem. Here they established the "Latin Kingdom of Jerusalem," with a feudal system of government. It was expected, however, that others would come to aid in the defense of the newly won territory and among those who did come were the Knights Hospitallers and Knights Templars, two newly formed military, monastic orders.

The Decline. As the years passed, the crusaders' control of the Holyland began to weaken. Disagreements with the Byzantine emperor were common. In addition, much of the earlier zeal was lost; too many of the crusaders accepted the ways of the East and lived a life of luxury. In the meantime the Turks were regaining their strength. Gradually they began to recover lost territory. In 1146 the *Second Crusade*, under the leadership of Emperor Conrad III and King Louis VII of France, set out for the Holyland to aid in its defense. But it was unsuccessful. The Turks were not driven back.

The King's Crusade. The situation soon became even more serious. Saladin, the Turkish leader, proclaimed a "Holy War" against the Christians and in 1187 he conquered Jerusalem. The defeat was a shock to all Europe. Immediately, a new crusade was formed under the leadership of Frederick Barbarossa, Philip II of France, and Richard the Lionhearted of England. But it was not very successful. Frederick Barbarossa drowned crossing a stream near Asia Minor in 1190. To make matters worse, Philip and Richard were mortal enemies. Philip thus returned to Europe after a short time, leaving Richard, a brave, dashing soldier but not a great general, in sole command. The crusade came to a rather unsatisfactory conclusion in 1192. The Turks agreed to a three year truce during which Christians could visit the Holyland, but they conceded nothing else.

The Errant Crusade. By now much of the spirit had gone out of the crusades. The result was that the next campaign was not a crusade at all. Instead of marching to the Holyland, the "crusaders," after attacking a Christian city along the Adriatic coast, took advantage of a quarrel in Constantinople and conquered the city in 1204. They then established a "Latin Kingdom" in the former Byzantine capital. Some attempts to heal the religious split between East and West were made, but in general, the Easterners were badly treated. Thus, when the Latin Kingdom fell in 1261 the Greeks had even more reason than before to hate the West.

Later Crusades. Some few attempts to regain the Holyland were made. The *Fifth Crusade,* proclaimed in 1215, was a miserable failure. St. Louis, King of France, led the *Sixth and Seventh Crusades,* but despite his greatness and piety no real success was achieved. Gradually, the movement came to an end and by 1291 all of the Christian holdings in the Near East had been regained by the Turks.

The Result. Militarily, the crusades were a failure. Yet, they were an eloquent testimony to the faith and religious zeal of Europe. Perhaps, however, this zeal was somewhat misdirected. For the first time, Christianity had attempted conquest on a mass scale, rather than conversion. The result did not bear out the efficacy of the change in tactics.

Medieval Missions

In comparison with earlier centuries there was relatively little missionary success in the later Middle Ages. Several factors account for this lack of success. For one thing, little was known about the non-European world and the possibilities of communication with the East were few. Moreover, the crusades took the dominant interest during the period. But missionary work was not wholly forgotten.

The Mohammedans. Some attempts to spread the Faith were made in conjunction with the crusades. St. Francis of Assisi, for example, visited the Mohammedan Sultan in Egypt and made a favorable impression. Some conversions were reported among Mohammedans, although they were not large in number compared to the total population. The Franciscans sent several missionaries to North Africa. But there were frequent martyrdoms and little success.

The Near East. The Mongols, a barbarian people from Mongolia, had swept into this area and were especially strong in Russia. Being pagans they did not share the prejudices of the Mohammedans. Thus in 1253 St. Louis of France sent several missionaries into Russia. They returned, however, without much success. Persia, another area held by the Mongols, seemed more promising. Some small success must have been achieved, for at one time the Franciscans had over nine mission houses in the country. Unfortunately, the Mohammedans later conquered the country and extinguished all traces of Christianity. Some Franciscans travelled all the way to China to win converts, but no lasting successful missions were established during this period.

Summary. No lasting success was therefore achieved by the missionaries of the twelfth and thirteenth centuries, but at least sufficient efforts had been made to demonstrate that the Church had not forgotten its obligation to extend the Faith to all lands.

The Church and Medieval Civilization

By the twelfth century a new stability had entered Europe. There was a revival of learning, of art, and of commerce. A new culture came into existence, a culture that was dominated by the Christian Faith. During this period all aspects of life were imbued with Christianity and the Church occupied the central place in medieval civilization.

The Church and Daily Life. The function of the Church is to save souls. To carry out this function the Church of the Middle Ages attempted to sanctify daily life and to bring it into close connection with the supernatural life. This was done in several ways.

Third Orders were founded as a result of the desire to allow lay people to share in the life of the religious orders. St. Norbert, founder of the Premonstratensians, began a Third Order which required the following of a modified rule and the wearing of a scapular as a sort of habit. It was St. Francis of Assisi, however, who was most important in this development. The famous Third Order of St. Francis required its members to pray frequently, to fast and abstain 3 days a week, to receive confession and Communion at least three times a year, and more than anything else, to participate in works of charity. Soon the Dominicans and other religious communities began their own Third Orders.

The Church also sought to sanctify the medieval

nobility by participating in the ceremony of knighthood. Candidates were required to fast for twenty-four hours, receive the sacraments, and to spend an all-night vigil before the Blessed Sacrament. The ceremony of knighthood itself was usually performed in church. In this way the Church sought to soften the cruelty of the nobility and to turn them into pious Christians and defenders of the Faith.

The world of business was also affected. Traders and artisans of the time grouped themselves into Guilds. Under the guidance of the Church, these soon took on religious functions. Members attended Mass in a body, prayed for their departed brethren, and assisted in works of charity. In addition, the Church constantly worked to achieve fair business practices. Cutthroat competition and high rates of interest, for example, were condemned by Church legislation.

The humble peasants were never far removed from the Church. The parish priest presided with the sacraments and services of the Church at important times in their lives: birth, marriage, and death. He blessed their fields and cared for them. Moreover, Church holydays afforded them rest from work and the opportunity for celebration.

Finally, the hand of the Church was evident in the many works of charity so necessary in medieval times. The Church, not the state, was primarily responsible for public welfare, the founding of hospitals, often called "Houses of God," and the care of the poor.

The Church and Culture. Art was very important in the medieval world, and here the work of the Church was pre-eminent. For the Church had the necessary wealth to actively support works of art. Moreover, the Church realized the value of art in leading souls to heaven. The typical medieval man, who could neither read nor write, learned what he knew of the Faith either from sermons, or from the pictures, statues, and stained glass windows in the churches. Thus, the art of the period was almost solely religious, and often a religious story was told in the panes of a window.

The greatest example of medieval Christian art was the Gothic cathedrals. Throughout Europe these magnificent buildings completely dominated the towns in which they were located—an eloquent testimony to the position of the Faith in medieval life. They were a sort of collective act of faith of a whole community, for each individual contributed his talents to the work.

The literature of the age was also predominantly religious. Even drama was used to instruct and edify the faithful. So-called mystery or mortality plays were performed on Christmas, Easter, or other special days. The lives of Christ, Mary, or the saints were favorite themes.

The Church and Intellectual Life. During the early Middle Ages all education had been in the hands of the Church. Only clerics were educated, and what schools existed were connected to monasteries or cathedrals. During this period, however, a new educational institution came into existence: the university. The universities were associations of students and teachers to carry on academic work. As such they were protected by the Church. Students were given the rights of the clergy: they were free, for example, from ordinary courts of law and could be tried only by Church courts, where sentences were usually lighter. Moreover, the education at the universities was basically Christian centered. Theology was accorded the position of "Queen of the Sciences." Other studies, however, were not neglected. The liberal arts, philosophy, medicine, and law were also studied.

The later Middle Ages was also a period of great advancement in Christian theology and philosophy. A system known as *Scholasticism* came into being. Basically, it was an attempt to take all knowledge, both human and divine, and to fuse it into one great intellectual system. It involved also a new approach to theology, that is, an attempt to make better use of philosophy in explaining and understanding the truths of the Christian religion. Thinkers such as St. Anselm, Abelard, Peter Lombard, and St. Albert the Great were important in the Scholastic movement. Most important of all, however, was St. Thomas Aquinas. His greatest work, the *Summa Theologica*, has remained a classic of Catholic theology down to the present day. While many criticized St. Thomas when he was alive and accused him of holding dangerous opinions, his canonization as a saint in 1323 silenced the opposition.

The Liturgy and Popular Devotions. The Church, of course, continued to make use of the more traditional and strictly religious means of leading souls to God. The liturgy was fairly stabilized by the twelfth century, but a few developments can be noted. For one thing the elevation of the Bread and Wine during the Mass was universally accepted. This was done partly to counteract the heresy of a certain Berengarius, who denied the real presence of our Lord in Communion. Benediction of the Blessed Sacrament also became common, largely for the same reason.

Popular devotions put great stress on the veneration of the Blessed Mother. In many areas the feast of the Immaculate Conception was celebrated, although some theologians such as St. Bernard questioned its validity. In addition, the use of the rosary came into prominence. The origins of this devotion are obscure, but it was soon popularized by the Dominicans with much success. The making of pilgrimages to the shrines of saints and the use of the Christmas crib were other popular devotions. The medieval man was also fond of sermons, which were usually excessively long, and wandering speakers and missionaries were very popular.

The Threat of Heresy

Despite the power of the Church, heresy continued to exist and, if anything, grew more serious. Moreover, the heresy of the age took on a peculiar characteristic: its dominant factor was almost always anticlericalism; that it, an attack on the position of the clergy. In some ways, this was a quite natural development since many of the old abuses still continued to exist. Thus, the door was left open for attacks on the lives of the clergy. Moreover, attacks on the evil lives of some clergymen led to attacks on the clergy in general. In addition, the very power of the Church gave rise to complaints. Even St. Bernard attacked the great wealth and splendor of the medieval papacy and bemoaned its increasing involvement in political affairs. Many asked if the great splendor of the Church was not somehow inconsistent with the poverty of Christ and His disciples. As a result of these factors, some heretical doctrines had a great appeal.

The Waldenses were the followers of a certain Peter Waldo, a wealthy French merchant of the late twelfth century. After becoming convinced that the holding of property was evil, he began to live in complete poverty. Soon he attracted followers who went around the countryside preaching, advocating poverty, and attacking abuses in the Church. But the group soon ran into trouble. Many of them were illiterate and as a result, local bishops often refused to permit them to preach. Waldo took his case to Pope Alexander III, who praised much of his work but forbade him to preach without the consent of the local bishop. After this the movement became more radical. Their criticism of abuses in the Church eventually led to attacks on the Church and clergy in general. Other heretical doctrines followed from

74

their private interpretation of the Bible. The Waldenses argued that all men are priests and that only baptism and communion were valid sacraments, the rest being mere inventions of the clergy. In 1184 they were excommunicated, although small groups continued to exist in many areas for a century or more.

The Albigensians were an even more serious threat. This heresy, a revival of the old Manicheaism, arose in the East as early as the seventh century and spread to the West by the eleventh century. Its stronghold became Southern France, where by the twelfth century it had developed a full-fledged organization with churches and bishops. The Albigensians believed in two gods, one of good and the other of evil. They believed further that all matter was evil since it was the creation of the evil god. Thus, they led a very rigorous life, eating no meat or dairy products and avoiding all material pleasures. Quite naturally the Albigensians attacked the Church. Moreover, they denied the lawfulness of oaths and this made them undependable in a feudal age so firmly based on oaths. Even more serious was their advocacy of suicide to avoid serious temptation. The Albigensians were condemned and excommunicated in 1119.

The War Against the Albigensians. The Church first tried the method of persuasion and conversion in dealing with heretics. St. Bernard and St. Dominic led missionary movements into southern France. But the situation continued to grow worse as the Albigensians began violently to attack Christian churches. The murder of a papal legate in southern France finally brought action. In 1208 Innocent III proclaimed a crusade against the Albigensians and some 200,000 knights led by Simon de Montfort advanced into the area. A hard and bitter campaign of twenty years followed, with much cruelty on both sides, but the heresy was finally crushed.

The Inquisition was another means used by the Church to combat heresy. This police force of the medieval Church had a twofold aim: to protect society from false teachings and to convert the heretics. After its establishment in the late twelfth century it was usually manned by Dominicans.

The procedure of the Inquisition was as follows: The Inquisitors would first come into a town and for a few days any heretic could come forward, admit his error, and receive only a light spiritual sentence. After this, however, the Inquisitors examined persons denounced to them as heretics. And, as was the fashion of the day, torture was used to obtain a confession. Those who confessed and repented were usually given light sentences. Proven heretics who refused to submit, however, were treated more severely: their property might be confiscated, they might be sent into exile or imprisoned, and, in certain instances, they were turned over to the state to be burned at the stake. Contrary to what some have claimed, however, the death sentence was given in only a small percentage of the cases.

It is difficult, if not impossible, to defend the Inquisition fully. It can, however, be explained. People in the Middle Ages looked upon heresy as one of the greatest sins. They also considered it a crime, for it amounted to treason against the Church in an age when the great majority of men accepted the teachings of the Church. To teach heresy was to undermine the whole fabric of medieval society and even before the establishment of the Inquisition there was much popular violence against heretics. Thus, the use of the Inquisition is understandable as a natural development of the times. Yet, in the final analysis, it may well be questioned whether it is either a very sensible or a very Christian practice to imprison and kill men for their beliefs, no matter how false they might be.

Conclusion

The later Middle Ages was one of the greatest periods in the history of the Catholic Church. The greatness of the Church did not lie, however, in the political victories of the papacy. These were only an unfortunate necessity, unfortunate because they gave rise to resentment and future difficulty, but necessary because without them the Church would not have been free to carry on its true function. For despite its concern with political affairs, the Church did not lose sight of its real task. The popular devotion of the people, so well demonstrated in the enthusiasm behind the Crusades and the Gothic cathedrals, the great numbers of saints, and vocations to the religious life all serve to demonstrate the spiritual achievements of the Church. Nor did the Church forget its obligations to society. The patronage of art, the advancement of learning, and the cultivation of a better life for all was also the work of the Church. Thus, the Church of the Middle Ages demonstrated that the real task for most Christians is not so much to renounce the world, as it is to transform the world in accordance with the teachings of Christ.

STUDY QUESTIONS

1. Contrast the papacy as you know it to be today with the papacy you read about during the "Age of Faith."
2. Contrast the spirit of faith as found in the Crusades with the spirit of faith found in the medieval missions.
3. How did the medieval Christian scholar show his reverence for the message of Christ?
4. Compare the power of the Church of God in the world of the twelfth and thirteenth centuries with that of the Church today.
5. Compare the freedom of action of the Church today

with the freedom of the Church in the twelfth and thirteenth centuries.

Bibliography

Belloc, Hilaire. *The Crusades: The World's Debate.* (Milwaukee: 1937).
(A good, short, readable summary.)
Chesterton, Gilbert Keith. *St. Francis of Assisi.* (New York: 1924).
———. *St. Thomas Aquinas.* (New York: 1933).
(Two very excellent biographies by a great Catholic author.)
Clayton, Joseph. *Pope Innocent III.* (Milwaukee: 1941).
(A good biography of the most powerful of the medieval popes.)
DeWohl, Louis. *The Joyful Beggar, a Novel of St. Francis of Assisi.* (Philadelphia: 1958).
———. *The Quiet Light, a Novel.* (Philadelphia: 1950).
(Two very readable works. The second is a biography of St. Thomas Aquinas.)
Jarrett, Bede. *Life of St. Dominic.* (Westminster, Md.: 1947).
(A good biography.)
Morison, James C. *The Life and Times of St. Bernard.* (London: 1863).
(A good biography of one of the greatest churchmen of the Middle Ages.)

Chapter IV

The Church in the Age of Transition

CHRIST CONTINUES TO LIVE IN HIS PEOPLE

Introduction

EUROPE in the fourteenth and fifteenth centuries went through an Age of Transition. Medieval culture was breaking down and modern culture was in its infancy. In every phase of life there was a process of decay and growth, as old ideas gave way to new. Inevitably the Church was affected by this transition, because it had so well identified itself with medieval life that it found it difficult to adjust to the new situation. Thus, the Age of Transition was an age of decline for the Church. Buffeted by outside forces it could no longer control, it also suffered an internal decay. Before examining the history of the Church in this difficult age, however, it is necessary to note briefly some of the new forces that were changing the world.

The Forces of Change

Economic Changes. The economic system of the Middle Ages was based on agriculture, with land as the real standard and source of wealth. By the fourteenth century, however, commerce and trade were becoming more important and as a result, money—gold and silver—became the new standard of wealth. As a consequence, land lost much of its former value. While the medieval Church was a wealthy institution, most of its wealth was in land. As a result, the Church found itself short of funds at the very time when increased functions demanded more and more revenue. In the fourteenth and fifteenth centuries, the Church was forced to find new means of getting money and these led to abuses and much resentment.

Social Changes. The Age of Transition was an age of great social upheaval. Numerous disasters brought about an increase of suffering and tension. A great number of peasant revolts occurred. The long Hundred Years War between France and England brought much distress. Between 1315 and 1317 there was widespread famine. Finally, the Black Death, a great plague which lasted from 1347 to 1350, killed at least ten million people. A large number of these were priests, who had to be replaced by insufficiently educated candidates.

More significant than any of these changes, however, was the rise of a new social class: the bourgeoisie or middle class. These were the traders and businessmen of the age. While they were not openly hostile to the Faith, many of their attitudes conflicted with the teachings of the Church. Men of wealth, they resented the superior social position of the nobility and the clergy. Men anxious to accumulate even more wealth, they attacked the influence which the Church exercised on the world of business.

Intellectual Changes. The scholastic system of the Middle Ages was crumbling. Its greatest thinkers were now dead. New lines of thought were being pursued, and some of these were dangerous. St. Thomas Aquinas had held that the truths obtained from reason could never contradict the truths revealed by the Faith. But the new thought, called Nominalism, denied this. William of Occam, the most prominent of the Nominalists, stated that there often was contradiction between faith and reason, and in so doing he undermined the intellectual foundation of the Faith.

It is significant, too, that intellectual leadership was passing out of the control of the Church. No longer was the clergy the only educated class. The middle class was also becoming educated, and they were anxious to overthrow the priority of sacred studies in the interest of more "practical" things.

Political Changes. Feudalism, as a political system, had also broken down. Instead of government by local nobles, monarchs were beginning to assume more and more power. Moreover, these monarchs were very jealous of their powers and greatly resented the intrusion of papal influence into what they considered to be their own affairs. Significantly, the people, and especially the middle class, were tired of the rule of the nobility and gave their support to the monarchs. At the same time, nationalism was on the rise: people began to think of themselves as Frenchmen, or Germans, or Englishmen, rather than as Christians who happened to reside in France, or Germany, or England. There was a tendency to distrust other nations. Frenchmen, for example, were not inclined to overly respect the decisions of an "Italian" pope.

All these changes, therefore, created a world in which the Church found it difficult to live.

The Quarrel of Boniface VIII and Philip IV

After the death of Frederick II in 1250 the political power of the papacy seemed assured. Yet there were signs of difficulty. A forty-year struggle for control of southern Italy seriously drained the resources of the papacy. Even greater trouble was ahead. The challenge did not come, however, from the empire, but from the powerful king of France, Philip IV.

Boniface VIII was elected pope in 1294. A capable Church lawyer and administrator, he was absolutely determined to maintain the political power of the papacy. Unfortunately, he was arrogant and stubborn, and alienated many cardinals and some of the most powerful families in Italy.

Trouble from France was not long in coming. As the result of the war with England, Phillip IV was in desperate need of money. He decided, therefore, to tax the clergy in a manner that was forbidden by Church law. When some of the French clergy appealed to Rome for protection, Boniface issued the famous Bull, *Clericus Laicos*. In this document he threatened that anyone who either paid or collected such an illegal tax was subject to automatic excommunication. Philip, however, was not deterred. In retaliation, he ordered that no money could be sent out of France. This was a terrible blow to the pope, himself in need of money, since the papacy received many taxes from the French Church. Boniface was forced to back down and conceded Philip's right to tax the clergy, in fact if not in theory.

The Quarrel Continues. The struggle began again in 1301 when Philip arrested the papal legate in France, after he had spoken critically of the royal chancellor. This again was a violation of Church law and several times Boniface warned Philip to amend his ways. The king only shot back angry replies. Then in 1302 Philip called a meeting of the French Estates General. Ominously, the Estates and a great number of the clergy supported the king. Boniface replied with *Unam Sanctum,* in which he warned the king that no one could obtain salvation unless he obeyed the pope. The document, however, was confusing. Was Boniface speaking merely of spiritual matters or was he also claiming political authority over the king? Philip assumed that he was claiming political authority. The climax came in 1303 as Boniface prepared to excommunicate the king. In September, Nogaret, the royal chancellor, and certain Italian enemies of the pope, took Boniface captive at the town of Anagni where he was staying. Defenders of the pope soon rallied their forces and the next day the pope's captors released him and fled. But Boniface, broken in spirit, died in October of 1303.

Philip's Victory. The next pope, Benedict XI (1303-4) was anxious to avoid trouble. Thus, he pardoned Philip and restored his privileges. Pope Clement V (1305-14), himself a Frenchman, went even further. The king was allowed to bring charges against the dead Boniface, and although the pope was found innocent, his reputation was permanently damaged. To complete the surrender, Clement then allowed Philip to abolish and confiscate the property of the Knights Templars, despite no wrongdoing on their part. The political power of the papacy was greatly weakened.

The Avignon Papacy

From 1309 to 1376 the popes were absent from Rome. During this period they resided instead at Avignon, a papal territory within France. The explanation of this departure from tradition is twofold. In the first place, French influence in the College of Cardinals was dominant after the death of Boniface VIII. Thus, all the popes elected in this period were French and they quite naturally preferred to remain close to their homeland. In the second place, the political situation in Rome was unusually bad. After 1303 the turbulent Roman nobles cast off the authority of the pope and carried on a virtual civil war for control of the city. Then in 1347 the Roman populace, under the leadership of the adventurous Cola di Rienzi, rose up and established a republic. In the midst of such confusion the city of Rome was hardly a safe residence for the popes.

Papal Government during the period was a mere continuance of trends already under way. The power of the Papal Curia continued to increase. By the end of the period the popes were appointing almost all the bishops in the Church and the old method of election was largely neglected. This change caused much resentment, however, and, in England especially there were efforts to resist it. As financial matters were a continual cause for concern, the machinery for the collection of taxes was overhauled and the number of taxes increased. Bishops, for example, were required to pay one-third of a year's income when they were appointed to that office. Since most of these taxes fell eventually on the laity there was again much resentment.

The Avignon Popes were mixed in quality. All were good administrators, some attempted to be reformers, and two of them have been beatified. But no matter who was pope, the political power of the papacy continued to decline. As of old, trouble was brewing in Germany. In 1314 a squabble developed when two different men each claimed to be emperor. Finally Louis of Bavaria secured recognition. Louis, however, soon angered the papacy because of his obvious interest in the affairs of northern Italy. As a result, Pope John XXII claimed that Louis was not the true emperor since the pope had never given his approval. When Louis refused to step down, John excommunicated him. Developments followed the normal pattern. Louis marched into Rome and set up his own man as pope in 1328. But Louis was overthrown by the German nobles in 1346 and apparently the papacy had again triumphed over its old enemy.

Such, however, was not the case. Ten years later Emperor Charles IV issued the so-called Golden Bull to establish for all time the method of electing emperors. Significantly, nothing at all was said about any necessity for the pope to approve the election. Pope Innocent VI vainly protested this arrangement, but to no avail. The papacy was thus curtly informed that its political power in Germany was a thing of the past. Papal power had suffered yet another defeat.

Reaction to the Avignon Papacy was almost universally unfavorable. Most Europeans suspected, although it was not really true, that the popes were completely under the thumb of the French monarchy. Moreover, there were constant complaints, partly justified, that the money flowing into Avignon was being wasted on luxury in the Papal Curia. Even such holy women as St. Brigid of Sweden and St. Catherine of Sienna bluntly told the popes of their duty to return to Rome.

The Return to Rome. For a long time the popes had been trying to return. In 1353 Pope Innocent VI sent Cardinal Albornoz into Italy at the head of a papal army to restore order. By 1354 the great soldier-cardinal had recovered Rome, and ten years later order was restored to almost all Italy. Taking advantage of these victories, Pope Urban V returned to Rome in 1367. But Albornoz soon died and Rome again became unsafe. Thus in 1370 Urban retraced his steps to Avignon and died there. The next pope, Gregory XI, decided to make another attempt after ardent encouragement from St. Catherine of Sienna. Another papal army, this time under the leadership of

Cardinal Robert of Geneva, was sent into Italy. Cardinal Robert did his work well, if somewhat roughly, and Gregory left Avignon in September of 1376. In January of 1377 he entered Rome and the Avignon Papacy was at an end. But within a year Gregory was dead and the situation in Rome was still far from encouraging.

The Great Western Schism

The Election. Ten days after the death of Gregory XI the College of Cardinals, most of whom were French, met to choose a new pontiff. The situation in Rome was one of disorder. A large mob had gathered to demand the election of a Roman, or at least an Italian. The situation grew worse when the mob invaded the papal wine cellars for refreshment and then almost broke into the election chamber itself. As all this was going on, the worried cardinals elected Bartolomeo Prignano, an Italian archbishop. Not sure that their choice would meet the approval of the mob, however, the cardinals decided on a temporary ruse. Against his will, the old Roman, Cardinal Tibaldeschi, was clothed in papal garments and thrust out on to the balcony as if he had been elected. Taking advantage of the resulting confusion, the cardinals escaped into hiding. Things soon cooled down, however, and when the truth became known, the Romans decided that they had done well enough by getting an Italian. The cardinals emerged from hiding and on April 18, 1378, Archbishop Prignano was crowned as Pope Urban VI with the cardinals in attendance.

The Schism. The cardinals soon discovered that they had made a terrible mistake. Before his election Prignano had been a capable administrator in the papal government. His reputation was blameless and he was known as something of a reformer. Once he became pope, however, his character changed. Constantly berating the cardinals—whose lives were not blameless to be sure—

Urban VI merely succeeded in angering them without doing any real good. The reforms he attempted to impose were unusually severe and did not touch the real abuses. He ordered, for example, that the cardinals should be allowed only one meal a day. By summer the cardinals had had enough. Making their way out of Rome, they gradually gathered at the city of Anagni.

In August they declared that the election of Urban had been invalid because of the threats imposed upon them by the Roman mob. In September they proceeded to "elect" Cardinal Robert of Geneva as pope. He took the name of Clement VII and set up his residence at Avignon.

Confusion in the Church. No matter what were the failings of Urban VI's character, the cardinals had acted incorrectly. Modern historians agree that the election of Urban VI was valid. Indeed, the actions of the cardinals themselves proved the validity of his election. By their attendance at his coronation and by their acceptance of favors and appointments from him, they demonstrated that they considered him the true pope. But to the man of the times the matter was not so simple.

Both sides presented a convincing case and even saints were in disagreement as to who was really pope. The result of the schism was, then, one of unlimited confusion. As each "pope" appointed his own cardinals, bishops, and other officials, no one knew whom to obey. Generally, the different European countries made their choice on the basis of political considerations. France and her ally, Scotland, as well as Spain, backed the Avignon claimant. England, Germany, Italy, and most of the other nations favored the Roman pope.

Attempts at Settlement. When Urban and Clement died, their cardinals each elected successors. But neither side could gain the recognition of all Christendom, nor could either defeat the other by military means. It seemed that the dispute would never end. Finally, the University of Paris was called upon to provide a solution. It suggested several alternatives, the last of which called for the meeting of a Church council to decide the question. As a result, cardinals of both sides abandoned their respective popes and met together at the Council of Pisa in 1409. Once there, the cardinals proceeded to depose the two men then claiming to be pope, although neither of them admitted the power of the council to do so. Then, they "elected" a new pope who took the name Alexander V. The problem, however, was not solved; it had only been made more complicated. Instead of two "popes," there were now three: a Roman pope, an Avignon pope, and a Pisan pope.

The Council of Constance (1414–18), meeting under the protection of the Emperor Sigismund, finally ended the schism. It began by deposing the Pisan pope, by now the successor of Alexander V. The Roman pope, the legitimate claimant, resigned after he had been allowed to officially convoke the council. The Avignon "pope" was then deposed and although he refused to accept the decision, he was left without any support. With the way now cleared, the council elected Martin V in 1417, the first pope for some thirty-nine years to be recognized by the whole Church. At the same time, the Council of Constance attempted to carry out a much needed reform of the Church. But here, little, if any, success was achieved.

Conciliarism, a doctrine which holds that a Church council is superior to the pope and that only a council can define the true teachings of the Church, was the next threat to the position of the papacy. As early as 1324 a certain Marsiglio of Padua had defended this doctrine. For a while it was only a theory, but the confusion of the Great Western Schism, the bad light that it threw on the papacy, and the fact that a council had to eventually solve it, made the theory of Conciliarism seem more reasonable. As a result, many prominent churchmen were soon defending the idea. The Council of Constance lent its weight to the theory by ruling that a Church council must meet every few years. Pope Martin V resisted the doctrine, however, and refused to approve such legislation. Nonetheless, the next pope, Eugene IV (1431–47), was faced with a serious crisis. The Council of Basle (1431–49) challenged the authority of the pope on several matters and finally attempted to depose him. But the council was unable to hold its ground and was finally forced to submit. Thus, the challenge to the spiritual authority of the papacy had been temporarily defeated. Significantly, however, the Protestant Revolt was only sixty-eight years away when the Council of Basle was finally forced to adjourn.

The Church and the Renaissance

Nature of the Renaissance. During the fifteenth century a movement known as the *Renaissance* reached its height. On the one hand, it was a "rediscovery" of the intellectual and artistic works of the ancient world. But the Renaissance was more than this, and some of its elements were dangerous for the Church. Intellectually, the Renaissance denounced the scholastic philosophy of the Middle Ages. Since the system was already in decay there was much to denounce, but unfortunately the good was thrown out with the bad. Economically, the Renaissance put great stress on the making of profit and unlimited greed often resulted. Politically, the age was an exceptionally violent one—political murder was so common as to evoke little comment. Nicholo Machiavelli, the great political theorist of the period, held that a ruler need not be bound by the moral law, and few of them were. In short, much paganism and immorality returned

89

with ancient art and literature. In the final analysis, the Renaissance was a revival of secularism—that is, an undue emphasis on the pleasures of this life to the exclusion of the spiritual life.

The Christian Renaissance. From the beginning the Church attempted to channel the Renaissance in a Christian direction. The popes were constant patrons of art and literature and the great works of Leonardo de Vinci and Michelangelo resulted. Men such as Erasmus of Rotterdam and St. Thomas More turned the achievements of the Renaissance into the service of the Faith. Erasmus, for example, made use of the better knowledge of Greek and Latin to turn out splendid translations of the New Testament and the writings of the early Church Fathers. But despite all this the Renaissance was never fully Christianized.

The Renaissance papacy lasted from 1447 to 1517, and some ten popes reigned during the period. Never has the quality of papal leadership been so poor from a spiritual point of view. Most of them were excellent politicians: indeed, they had to be, for Italy was in a state of turmoil as the Empire, France, and Spain all struggled to control it. All of them encouraged Renaissance arts and letters, sometimes to the exclusion of more pressing spiritual concerns. Most of them were frivolous and loved luxury. All too often the papal court seemed little different from any other royal court. Many were more interested in increasing the fortunes of their families than in the welfare of the Church. But worst of all, a few of these popes were openly immoral. Most infamous of the ten was Pope Alexander VI (1492–1503). With such conditions, it is little wonder that the prestige of the papacy suffered even further decline.

Abuses in the papal government quite naturally grew serious. A great number of these abuses stemmed from the popes' desire to enrich their own families, or from political reasons. The most serious ones involved the appointment of bishops and other officials. *Simony,* the attempt to sell a spiritual office, was again cropping up and the use of bribery in papal elections was not unknown. *Nepotism,* the appointing of one's relatives to office was all too common. *Commendation* was the practice of appointing someone under age to an official position. Pope Alexander VI, for example, had been an official in the Papal Curia at the age of thirteen. *Pluralities* was the practice of allowing one man to hold several offices at the same time. It sometimes happened that one man became the bishop of four or five dioceses. The natural result of this was *absenteeism;* that is, absence from one's duties. Some churchmen, for example, had never even been in the diocese of which they were bishop. They simply collected the revenue. All these abuses led to the neglect of the faithful.

Administrative Anarchy. The abuses which Savonarola criticized were due in large part to the lack of proper organization of the Church's administration. The Gregorian reforms had by-passed the bishops and put full power and responsibility in the hands of the pope and his curia. This centralization was satisfactory as long as the popes were capable men. But central administration broke down during the Great Schism, and it was not repaired by the popes of the Renaissance.

Bishops were unable to correct abuses, because they were not masters in the dioceses. In every diocese there were monasteries, congregations, and priories free from episcopal supervision, as were most pastors. In Paris, the bishop appointed only one out of every five pastors. Most of the others were appointed by laymen, and were not responsible to the bishop.

Monastic orders were in no better condition. Many monasteries cut loose from their General Chapter and became completely independent. They were often under absentee abbots who were interested only in the monastery's income, and appointed a local monk to act in their place. Often the abbot was a layman who had no interest in religious life.

Critics of the clergy soon arose to attack such conditions. Nor was the criticism confined to the papacy and the hierarchy. The monasteries had lost much of their vigor and suffered a decline. Erasmus, for one, hotly denounced the all too frequent monks who concentrated on such trivia as the proper cut of their habit while neglecting their more serious duties. Nor were the parish clergy in good condition. Violations of the law of celibacy were again occurring, and the ignorance of many of the clergy formed material for endless jokes and barbs.

Among the many critics, one man took action. This was Jerome Savonarola (1452–98), a Dominican monk who denounced the evil lives of clergy and laity alike in his native Florence. Eventually he took over control of the city. But Savonarola went too far. Even innocent amusements were forbidden under his rule, and children were encouraged to spy on their parents. Soon he found himself in a political dispute with the papacy, and after being toppled from power in 1497, he was burned at the stake after receiving the sacraments. But if Savonarola was a fanatic, he was a fanatic who spoke much truth.

Religious Life in the Age of Transition

Religious Orders. The poor condition of the Church can partly be seen in the virtual lack of new religious orders during the period. The only new order of any real importance was the Brethren of Common Life, founded by Gerard Groote in the last half of the fourteenth century. While the rule called for a community life, it did not require the taking of any vows. The Brethren did much good work, however, especially in the care and education of children. The order also fostered much popular devotion. *The Imitation of Christ* by Thomas à Kempis, which is still popular today, was written by a member of the Brethren. But no order capable of fully reforming the Church appeared.

The Missions. Even in its darkest hours the Church did not neglect its responsibility to spread the Faith. In 1269 Marco Polo returned to Italy from China and knowledge of the Far East was available. As a result, Pope Nicholas IV sent a certain friar, John of Montecorvino, to China in 1294. As China was then ruled by the Mongols, toleration was extended to Christian missionary work. By 1299 Friar John had built a church in the great city of Peking and soon other missionaries joined him. By 1328 it is estimated that over 30,000 converts had been won. Unfortunately, decline set in after this. Then in 1368 the Mongols were overthrown by native Chinese rulers and a persecution of Christians began.

The Liturgy. Although there were no significant changes in the Mass or the sacraments, the feasts of Corpus Christi and the Blessed Trinity were extended to the universal Church. One disturbing note, however, was the less frequent reception of Holy Communion by the faithful.

Popular devotion remained very strong, for ordinary people were still closely attached to the Faith. Penitential preachers, who constantly urged reform, were very popular. Devotion to the Passion of Our Lord showed itself in the introduction of the Stations of the Cross. Christian respect for the Blessed Mother continued to grow and the *Angelus* came into use about this time. Finally, devotions in honor of St. Joseph were extremely popular.

But there were serious abuses. Too often religious practices became mechanical, a mere going through the motions. Many pilgrimages, for example, were little more than holiday excursions. At the same time there was a tendency to excess. Periods of terrible immorality were followed by periods of excessive and sometimes almost inhuman penance. The great disorders of the age led to an obsession with death and the darker side of life. As a consequence, superstition, the result of ignorance and fear, was all too common. The real beginnings of witch-craft hysteria, for example, were found in these years. At the same time, however, there were attempts to better educate the laity. Numerous catechisms and prayer books, made possible by the invention of printing, did some good.

Heresy remained a serious problem. An English priest, John Wyclif (1324–84), after attacking the lives of many clergymen, held that it was evil for the Church to own any property at all. Eventually, he denied the spiritual authority of pope and bishops and rejected the power of the sacraments. Although his teachings were condemned in 1382, a group of his followers, known as Lollards, remained strong for many years.

The ideas of Wyclif soon made their way to Europe. There they were taken up by John Hus (1369–1415), a Bohemian priest who attracted many followers. Anxious to obtain approval of his ideas, Hus journeyed to the Council of Constance after being granted a "safe conduct." But the emperor warned him that he would not be protected if he was found to be in error. After examining the ideas of Hus, the Council condemned them. Hus, who refused to recant, was burned at the stake in 1415, but his ideas did not die with him. A group of followers kept them alive. The Church, tainted by abuses, was finding it more and more difficult to repress heresy.

Conclusion

Never, perhaps has the history of the Church been more dismal than it was in the Age of Transition. Dominated by the state and too often led by faithless and incapable rulers, its influence on society constantly declined. Yet one must not condemn the Church, only those who were responsible for its decline, and even these must be understood, and perhaps forgiven, for they lived in a difficult age. Nor was the history of the Church in this period all black. The teachings of Christ were maintained and the grace of the sacraments was available to all. The Faith produced saints and reformers even if they were not listened to, and missionary work was attempted. Again the history of the Church in the Age of Transition offers proof of the power of God. If the Church is to thrive, the co-operation of man is required; but even if man chooses for the moment not to co-operate, God will preserve His work.

STUDY QUESTIONS

1. What developments in the secular world exerted pressure on the life of the Mystical Body during the centuries of transition?
2. How did the Christian people react to the changes of the time of transition?
3. How vital was the presence of Christ in the community of His disciples during the Age of Transition? Illustrate.
4. What areas of the life of the Church needed reform at this time? List them in the order of their importance and give a reason for the order.
5. How would you describe the relationship of clergy and laity at this time in history?
6. Where do you find the continuing presence of the Savior in His people in this age?
7. Which of the previous periods in the Church's history would you think of as a time of transition? Why?
8. In what way is our time an age of transition in the Church? How does it compare with the period just before the Reformation?

Bibliography

Beas, T. S. *Boniface VIII.* (London: 1933).
(A good biography of the last of the great medieval popes.)

Dark, Sidney. *The Story of the Renaissance.* (New York: 1924).
(A short summary of this important period.)

DeWohl, Louis. *Lay Siege to Heaven, a Novel of St. Catherine of Sienna.* (New York: 1961).
(The life of a great saint who lived during the most difficult period in this history of the Church.)

Chapter V

The Age
of the
Reformation

CHRIST RE-CREATES AN
ACCEPTABLE PEOPLE

Introduction

BY THE beginning of the sixteenth century the Church was clearly in need of thorough reform and some small efforts in that direction were already underway. But before they could be brought to completion the Church suffered a serious loss. First in Germany, then in Switzerland, then in England, then indeed throughout all Europe, the Protestant Reformation broke forth. Before it was over, a large part of Europe was lost to the Faith. The Church was thus presented with a challenge to its spiritual authority more serious than at any previous time. But the Church did not retreat from this challenge. Instead, it proceeded to reform and renew itself and to begin the difficult task of winning back the great number of souls lost to the Faith.

Causes of the Reformation

Before beginning the complex story of the Reformation it would be well to mention briefly some of the factors which brought it about. It should be remembered that heresy was not a new thing; it had always existed. Thus, it is not surprising that heresy arose in the early sixteenth century. What is surprising and what needs to be explained is why this heresy was so successful and why it was accepted by so many people. The answer is not to be found solely in religious factors.

Intellectual Causes. As has been seen, secularism was continually on the rise. Man was becoming more interested in the things of this world and was neglecting his eternal destiny. The hold of the Church on men's minds was therefore weakened. At the same time, the decline of Christian thought and the rise of skepticism led many to doubt the teachings of the Church and thus prepared the way for revolt.

Political Factors were also important. Kings and princes of the different European countries were often resentful of the power and authority of the Church. Thus, they were tempted to support heresy as a way to overthrow and weaken that power. Moreover, many people, affected by nationalism, were suspicious of the "Italian" pope, and inclined to support their rulers, or any heretic who claimed to defend his country against the "interference" of the papacy.

Economic Causes had a very important place in the revolt. For one thing, the landed wealth of the Church was a prize worth the plucking. Both nobles, whose financial position was declining, and kings, who needed more and more money to finance their government, were tempted to adopt heresy, for by doing so they were given a ready-made excuse to confiscate Church lands.

Social Factors also played a part. The social conditions of the age were in a state of unrest, and the middle class was particularly anxious to increase its position in society. But too often it found that the superior position of the nobility was seemingly approved by the Church. The middle class resented this fact and sought a religion which would bless its way of life and end the old restrictions on the accumulation of wealth.

Religious Causes must not, however, be forgotten. The moral failings of many of the clergy and the many abuses in administration weakened the prestige of the Church. People were now more inclined to listen to so-called reformers who denounced not only the abuses, but the teachings of the Church as well. Moreover, the abuses had weakened the ability of the Church to oppose and challenge heresy in an effective manner.

Thus, conditions were ripe for a revolt by the early sixteenth century. Only a spark was needed to light the fires of revolution and that spark was provided by an obscure German priest in 1517.

Martin Luther and the German Revolt

The Early Life of Luther. Martin Luther was born at Eisleben, Germany, on November 10, 1483. His childhood was difficult: a violent father inflicted many beatings on him and a gloomy mother too often showed him the dark side of life. Yet he received a good education for his day. In 1501 he went to the University of Erfurt to study law. Several events occurred, however, which changed Luther's choice of a vocation. After narrowly recovering from a serious illness, he was shocked to learn of the sudden death of a close friend. Then, he was knocked off his horse by a bolt of lightning while returning to the university. In fear of his life, Luther called out to St. Anne to save him, and promised that if she did so he would become a monk. Later, Luther felt himself bound by this promise and, apparently without a

99

true religious vocation, he entered the Augustinian Order in July of 1505. Already well-educated, his rise in the clerical life was rapid. In 1507 he was ordained a priest and in 1512 he received a doctorate in theology and began to teach Sacred Scripture at the University of Wittenberg.

Luther's Religious Problem. Openly Martin Luther was an ordinary monk, even perhaps a brilliant one, but inside he was undergoing a religious crisis. Perhaps due to the influence of his mother, Luther was terrified at the vengeance of God. Continually worried about his salvation and afraid that his sins had not been forgiven, he repeated his confessions over and over again. His spiritual advisers were unable to quiet him, both because they refused to take him seriously and because Luther was apparently too stubborn to follow their directions.

In the midst of such turmoil Martin Luther came upon what was for him a significant discovery. In studying the Epistle of St. Paul to the Romans he came across the sentence: "The just man shall live by faith." This was the answer to his problem, for he interpreted it to mean that man is saved solely by his faith in Christ. Good works amount to nothing in the eyes of God, for man is sinful and can do no good. To be saved one need only believe that Christ has earned his salvation by His suffering and death and accept that salvation.

From this moment Martin Luther was a heretic, for he had denied the traditional Christian teaching that man must not only believe, but that he must also cooperate by his good works with the grace of God. But this heresy was not immediately apparent; only another crisis would bring it into the open.

The Indulgence Controversy. Luther's open break with the Church came as the result of an indulgence preached in Germany. An indulgence, of course, is the remission of the temporal punishment due to past sins, often granted by the Church when a person receives the sacraments and performs some designated good work. At the time of Luther, Pope Leo X, anxious to rebuild St. Peter's Cathedral, offered an indulgence to all who would contribute to the work, provided that they would fulfill the usual requirements. Subsequently, the indulgence was preached in Germany.

There were abuses, however. Part of the money so collected went to Archbishop Albert of Brandenberg so that he could pay off debts contracted in order to purchase a dispensation from the papacy to hold three dioceses at one time. In addition, the preacher of the indulgence, the Dominican John Tetzel, made certain inaccurate statements in his enthusiastic appeals. Luther immediately jumped to the attack. On October 31, 1517, he posted the famous 95 Theses on the church door at Wittenberg, challenging Tetzel to a debate, attacking indulgences and several other teachings of the Church. This action was reported to the papacy, but Leo X was too busy with other matters and let the issue slide.

The Split Grows. By 1518, however, the papacy was forced to take action. Cardinal Cajetan was sent to Germany to treat with Luther. For several days he listened patiently as Luther attacked the spiritual power of the pope. When Cajetan asked Luther to retract his false ideas, the latter refused. In 1519 Luther repeated his heretical ideas in a famous debate with John Eck, the Catholic champion.

The Revolt. In 1520 Luther published three important pamphlets attacking the power of the Church. In June of that same year, Leo X issued *Exsurge Domine* which condemned Luther's teachings and gave him sixty days to recant. Luther's answer came in December when he publicly burned the papal bull. Thus, on January 3, 1521, Martin Luther was excommunicated. All now depended on what action Emperor Charles V would take. In April of 1521 Luther was summoned before the Diet of Worms, where once again he refused to recant. Declared an outlaw, he was hidden by one of the German princes before the emperor could enforce the decision.

Lutheran Doctrine. For the next few years, Luther was busy translating the Bible into German and formulating his ideas. The major points of his doctrine should be mentioned.

First, Luther affirmed that salvation is by faith alone. Good works are of no value. Man is saved solely by believing in Christ and accepting His redemption.

Second, the Church has no real authority. It is only a free society of those who believe. The clergy have no sacramental powers and their only duty is to preach the gospel.

Third, the Bible is the only guide of what to believe, for the authority of the Church in matters of faith is of no consequence.

Fourth, all sacraments, except Baptism and Holy Communion, are mere inventions of the papacy. Only Baptism and Communion are necessary for salvation.

Fifth, monasticism and clerical celibacy are evil and need not be observed, an idea which Luther put into practice by marrying a former nun.

Finally, Luther taught that it was the duty of the state and the prince to guide and protect the Church, and thus he tended to subject the Church to the state.

The Spread of Lutheranism. Soon many princes, churchmen, and people accepted Luther's ideas. Even the peasants were at first attracted, but when Luther condemned their revolt against the nobles in 1524 they largely turned away from him. Emperor Charles V was a sincere Catholic and was anxious to crush the Lutheran heresy, but a war against France and fear of a Turkish invasion occupied most of his time. Moreover, these problems made it necessary for him to retain the support of the German princes, many of whom were Lutherans, and he hesitated to enforce the laws against heresy.

As time passed, there were some attempts to reunite Catholics and Lutherans. In 1530 Philip Melancthon, Luther's chief assistant, drew up the *Augsburg Confession* which minimized differences between the two groups. But when a reconciliation proved impossible, the Lutheran princes formed a league to protect themselves and much fighting occurred. The issue was still undecided.

The Survival of Lutheranism. By 1546 the emperor was finally free to take action against the Lutherans, and for a time he subdued the princes. But in 1551 the Lutherans again revolted. Thus, in 1555 the *Peace of Augsburg* provided that each prince could establish the official religion of his area, provided that it was either Lutheran or Catholic. Moreover, warfare between the two groups was to cease and there was to be no more confiscation of each other's property.

Lutheranism in Scandinavia. For reasons somewhat the same as those operating in Germany, Lutheranism also spread to the countries of Denmark, Norway, and Sweden. At the beginning of the sixteenth century, these three countries were all united under the kingdom of Denmark. Sweden, however, was anxious to gain its independence and the fact that Archbishop Trolle, the highest prelate in the land, opposed this turned many against the Church. When the revolt finally succeeded in 1523 the new king, Gustavus Vasa, confiscated the property of the Church to support his new government. Lu-

103

theran preachers were soon in the country and within a short time Lutheranism became the official religion of the state.

In Denmark and Norway, which remained united, a revolt also led to the overthrow of the Catholic Church. Frederick I, who came to power as the result of a revolt in 1523, also confiscated the lands of the Church and gave them to the nobles so that they would support him. The nobles, anxious to preserve their newly won property, turned to Lutheranism and it was soon imposed on the whole nation.

Summary. Thus, from the scruples of a German priest, a movement developed which for the first time permanently split the religious unity of Europe. Northern Germany and Scandinavia were lost to the Faith, and new heretical movements quickly arose in other lands.

John Calvin and International Protestantism

The revolt of Martin Luther was largely confined to Germanic Europe. Moreover, many of Luther's ideas were not yet fully developed. Protestantism required a leader to formulate a doctrine that would have a wider appeal. That leader soon appeared in the person of John Calvin, who made his influence felt in a nation that had already undergone a preliminary reformation.

The Revolt in Switzerland. At the same time as Luther, another man was beginning a similar revolt in Switzerland. Ulrich Zwingli, a Swiss priest, had long studied the ideas of Erasmus. His radical interpretation of such ideas, added to his great difficulty in observing church laws regarding celibacy, led him into the ranks of Protestantism. Becoming pastor of a church in Zurich in 1519, he began to attack various Catholic teachings. In 1522 he began a campaign to "reform" the Church in Zurich, and in 1523 the city council voted to accept his teachings. Soon other cities in Switzerland accepted Protestantism, and a war broke out when they attempted to impose these teachings on the country districts. Zwingli himself was killed in this struggle in 1531. But as in Germany, neither side could win, and the *Peace of Kappel* allowed each area to determine its own beliefs.

John Calvin soon added his weight to Swiss Protestantism. Born in 1509 of a French middle-class family, he was as different from Luther as a man could be. Where Luther was often emotional, Calvin was coldly logical. Calvin was raised a Catholic, but his father got into financial trouble with the Church and was excommunicated, an event which may have turned the young Calvin against the Church. He received a good education, however, and in 1531 he turned to the study of theology. By this time he had apparently accepted certain Protestant ideas and in 1533 he made an open break with the Church. An heretical speech, written by Calvin, and delivered by a friend of his at the University of Paris, was immediately condemned. Calvin was forced to flee and after wandering around France for several years, he eventually made his way to Switzerland.

Calvin's Religious Doctrine. In 1536 John Calvin published *The Institutes of the Christian Religion.* Later revised and enlarged, it contains his major ideas. Calvin's chief contribution was the doctrine of predestination. Agreeing with Luther that salvation is by faith alone, he struck out on his own by holding that faith is a free gift given by God to some men and denied to others. Thus, man can do nothing to achieve his own salvation; he is either saved or damned according to the eternal will of God. Like Luther, Calvin believed that the Bible is the only rule of religious truth, but he was more strict than Luther in his interpretation of Scripture. Calvin reduced the sacraments to mere symbols which have no power to aid in salvation, but only confirm the faith of the elect, or those whom God has chosen to save. The clergy, therefore, have no sacramental powers. Their sole task is to preach the Gospel, as interpreted by John Calvin. Finally, Calvin reversed Luther's opinion by holding that the state ought to be subject to the Church.

Calvin in Geneva. In August of 1536 Calvin passed through the Swiss city of Geneva, intending to stay there only overnight. The city was in a ferment. Attempting to win its independence from the Duke of Savoy, it had already accepted Protestantism under the leadership of William Farel. Farel persuaded Calvin to remain in Geneva and the two men were soon in control of the city. Their rule was so strict, however, that in 1538 a revolt drove them out. But unable to maintain order, the city fathers implored Calvin to return in 1541. After this he quickly established his church-dominated society. All former Catholic practices and even innocent amusements were forbidden. Those who disagreed with Calvin's ideas were punished or forced to leave. Michael Servetus, a Spanish heretic who denied the Trinity, was burned at the stake when he was discovered in the city in 1553. Thus, until his death in 1564 Calvin ruled as high priest over the "city of the elect."

The Appeal of Calvinism. It at first seems strange that men would have accepted the ideas of John Calvin. The thought of a God who arbitrarily condemns men to eternal damnation is not a consoling one. Nor do most men like to live in an environment where even innocent amusements are forbidden. Yet Calvinism was immediately popular and Protestants from all over Europe were soon coming to Geneva to study at the feet of the master.

Why was his religion so successful? In the first place, the strict morality of Calvin appealed to an age which deplored the pagan nature of Renaissance life. In the second place, Calvin's religion was coldly logical and

106

appealed to the reason of many men. But most importantly, the ideas of Calvin had an immediate attraction for the middle class. It stressed their virtues: the virtues of thrift, industry, and frugality. Moreover, it seemed to provide a divine blessing to the accumulation of wealth. To a Calvinist, anxious to discover if he had been granted salvation, it seemed quite logical that those who prospered on this earth would be favored in the next life. Thus, wealth became the sign of salvation. As a result, it was the middle class, more than any other group, who accepted and spread the ideas of John Calvin.

The Spread of Calvinism. In several areas of Europe Calvinism was tremendously successful. In Holland it grew very strong and played a large part in that country's successful revolution against the rule of Catholic Spain. In Scotland, too, it soon won the day. Preached by the ex-priest, John Knox, it was accepted by many Scottish nobles who used their power in Parliament to outlaw Catholicism in 1560, and then later to overthrow the Catholic queen of the country. In France Calvinism was long a serious threat to the Catholic faith. Even in Germany, Calvinism began to challenge both Lutherans and Catholics and brought about serious conflicts. Thus, Calvinism became international Protestantism, militant and strong.

The Reformation in England

In England, the Reformation was almost solely the work of the king. To be sure, there was some resentment of the power of the papacy. Moreover, the followers of John Wyclif and certain groups at the Universities of Oxford and Cambridge had accepted heretical doctrines. There were some abuses, but these were less serious than in most other areas of Europe. The great majority of the people were loyal to the Church, and there would have been no revolt without the active support of the crown.

The Divorce Question. Henry VIII became king of England in 1509. Extremely intelligent, he was nonetheless stubborn and unable to control his passions. Yet, he remained a Catholic. In 1521 the papacy awarded him the title "Defender of the Faith" when he wrote his *Defense of the Seven Sacraments* against the teachings of Luther. But soon a serious problem arose. Henry's wife was Catherine of Aragon, who had formerly been married to Henry's older brother. When he died, a dispensation was granted by the papacy so that Henry could marry her. By 1525, however, Henry had grown tired of Catherine. She had given him no male heir, and besides, the king had his eye on a certain Anne Boleyn.

The king thus sought to have his marriage to Catherine declared null and void, on the grounds that the Bible forbade anyone to marry his brother's wife, and that the papal dispensation was invalid. Henry expected no trouble. In 1527 when the case was brought before an English ecclesiastical court, Cardinal Wolsey, the papal legate in England and Henry's right-hand man, was set to declare the marriage null. But the other judge, Archbishop Warham, suggested that the case was doubtful and ought to be sent to Rome.

Thus, the difficult matter was thrown into the lap of Pope Clement VII, a weak and indecisive man. He knew that to refuse Henry would mean trouble for the English Church. At the same time, he hesitated to rule against Catherine, because she was a close relative of the powerful German emperor, Charles V. Thus, Clement hesitated, hoping that the matter would somehow take care of itself. In 1528, however, the pope appointed Wolsey and Cardinal Campeggio to hear the case in England. But in July of 1529 when all the evidence was in, Campeggio adjourned the court for six months, rather than render a decision.

Once again the case was sent back to Rome and Clement again hesitated. Using every weapon at his disposal,

Henry found it impossible to force Clement to render a favorable decision. Finally, the king took matters in his own hands. He had already been living with Anne Boleyn for some time, she was pregnant, and action was of the utmost importance. In May of 1533, Thomas Cranmer, the Archbishop of Canterbury and a secret Protestant, declared that Henry's marriage to Catherine was null and void and proceeded to marry Henry and Anne. The hand of Rome was thus forced, and in 1533 the papal marriage court ruled in favor of Catherine; Henry's marriage to Anne was declared invalid and the king was instructed to take back his first wife.

The English Schism. Henry was now forced to go further, and in 1534 a packed Parliament passed the *Act of Supremacy.* Declaring that the king was the supreme head of the Church in England, it required everyone to take an oath to that effect. Most did so, but a few men, such as Bishop John Fisher and Thomas More, refused and suffered martyrdom for the Faith. The English Church was thus separated from Rome. Soon Henry took other steps. Between 1536 and 1539 the monasteries in England were taken over by the crown and their lands confiscated. Much of this land was later given to nobles and members of the middle class, who now became definitely anti-Catholic in order to protect their property.

Henry's Religious System. Despite his break with Rome, Henry was determined to uphold Catholic doctrine. The Mass, the seven sacraments, and the traditional teaching on almost all other matters were maintained, although many of the king's advisers wanted to go further. But when Henry died in 1547 the English Church was only in schism; heresy was yet to come.

Edward VI and Heresy. Edward VI was Henry's son by his third marriage and was only ten years old when his father died. Thus, the government was controlled by regents. Most important for religious matters, however, was Thomas Cranmer. Under his leadership England soon adopted heresy. The Mass was replaced by a service based on Cranmer's *Second Book of Common Prayer*, the use of which was made obligatory by the Act of Uniformity in 1552. The 42 Articles Act of 1553 was clearly Protestant in tone. All sacraments but Baptism and Communion were denied, and the real presence of Our Lord in Communion was also rejected. But how long could Protestantism survive? Edward, a very sickly boy, died in 1553, and the heir to the throne was Mary Tudor, the daughter of Henry and Catherine of Aragon, a devoted Catholic.

Queen Mary and the Catholic Revival. Despite an attempt to deprive her of the throne, Mary became queen in 1553. She then quickly moved to restore England to the Church. A new Parliament was persuaded to repeal all of the heretical legislation of Edward VI, and after the Church agreed not to demand the surrender of the land stolen from the monasteries, the schism was ended. On November 30, 1554, Cardinal Pole, the papal legate to England, received the country back into the Church.

But Mary's success was short lived for she made many mistakes. Her marriage to Philip II, the king of Spain, was unpopular. Her persecution of Protestants, in which some 273 persons, including Cranmer, were burned at the stake, was a needless and unpopular act. Finally, unable to have children, she died in 1558 leaving the throne to Elizabeth, the daughter of Anne Boleyn.

The Establishment of Protestantism. Queen Elizabeth was quite naturally anti-Catholic because of the Church's condemnation of her mother's marriage to Henry. But, in reality, Elizabeth and her adviser, William Cecil, were more interested in power than in religion and they believed that Protestantism would better serve their purpose. In 1559, therefore, Parliament reversed itself, and passed another Act of Supremacy making Elizabeth the supreme governor of the Church in England. At the same time, *The Book of Common Prayer* was restored and in 1563 the *39 Articles Act* gave England a set of religious doctrines that were clearly Protestant. In 1570 Pope St. Pius V excommunicated the queen and declared her deposed. But her power remained firm. A long persecution of Catholics and priests began and the Faith was successfully destroyed in England.

Summary. Thus, after a century of confusion, England was lost to the Faith, a loss that was especially serious since that country was eventually to become the most powerful in the world and to control a large colonial empire.

The Catholic Reformation

At the same time as the Protestant Revolt was occurring, a true reformation was being carried out by the Church; a reformation that would purify and strengthen her for the battle ahead.

Early Reform Efforts. Even during the worst period of the Church there were some efforts at reform. In Spain, Cardinal Ximines, with the co-operation of Ferdinand and Isabella, reformed the clergy and corrected abuses. In Rome, Pope Julius II (1503-13) called the *Fifth Lateran Council* which passed some legislation against abuses. Unfortunately, however, these regulations were largely ignored, and Julius was too busy with other matters to enforce them. But by this time, there were men determined to do more. A group known as the *Oratory of Divine Love* worked hard to Christianize the Renaissance and to spiritualize daily life. Then, in 1524 an order known as the *Theatines* was formed. Its goal was to produce priests who would do simply what priests

111

were supposed to do: preach and administer the sacraments. Both of these groups provided numerous reformers to the Church.

The Reformed Papacy. No true reform, however, could be carried out without the strong leadership of the papacy. By the time that Leo X, the last of the Renaissance popes, died in 1521 the Protestant Revolt was in the open. Thus, his successor, Adrian IV (1522-23), was determined to take action. Admitting the existence of abuses in the Church, he attempted to carry out a reform. But Adrian's rough mannerisms angered many, and his reign was too short for any real success. The next pope, Clement VII (1523-34) was both too weak and too busy with the English revolt to take action. But in 1534, the papacy received the leader it so desperately needed.

Pope Paul III had led an immoral life as a youth, but having reformed himself, he was fully devoted to the reform of the Church and possessed the ability to carry it out. His first step was to appoint new cardinals favorable to reform, for the opposition of the College of Cardinals was a serious weakness. Then he appointed the famous *Commission of Nine* to investigate abuses in the Church. Its report of 1537 bluntly attacked the evil lives of clergymen and such abuses as simony, pluralism, absenteeism, and nepotism. Moreover, it informed the Papal Curia that it had been responsible for many of the weaknesses of the Church. Pope Paul immediately carried out the recommendations of the Commission; the Curia was reformed, abuses were curbed, and bishops were ordered to return to their dioceses. At the same time, Paul was anxious to call a general council to reform the entire Church.

The Calling of the Council. For a long time, a council had been desired, but many factors prevented its meeting. The papacy, afraid of conciliarism, had hesitated to convoke a council. Many rulers and churchmen had also

112

opposed a council because they knew that the reform of abuses might conflict with their personal interests. Moreover, there were vast physical difficulties in gathering so many men together at one time. But Paul would listen to no excuses and, after several failures, he issued a call for a council to meet at Trent. After much difficulty the council finally convened in December of 1545.

The council's procedure was such that conciliarism was prevented. The pope was represented by legates, who presided over the council and who alone could introduce matters for discussion. Only bishops, abbots, and the heads of religious orders were allowed to vote, although Church lawyers and theologians could advise and state their opinions. Moreover, all legislation had to be sent to the papacy for final approval.

The Course of the Council. The first meeting of the council lasted from 1545 to 1547. After accomplishing a great deal, it was brought to an end by the outbreak of a plague in Trent and the partial opposition of Emperor Charles V. The new pope, Julius III (1550-55), called the second meeting of the council in 1551. A group of Protestant theologians came to Trent, but no reconciliation was possible. Then, a revolt against Charles V threatened the council and the second meeting came to an end in 1552. After this there was a lull. Pope Paul IV (1555-59) was a determined reformer, but he had little use for councils. His manner was extremely rough and he made many enemies, but his righteous anger put the fear of God into all those guilty of abuses. His successor, Pope Pius IV (1559-65), was, however, anxious to recall the council and did so in 1562. This third meeting completed the remaining work and the council was finally adjourned in 1563. Then, on January 26, 1564 Pius IV approved all the decrees of the council.

The Accomplishments of the Council. The task of the council was twofold: first, it had to define true Catholic

113

doctrine in the face of Protestant error; and second, it had to carry out a disciplinary reform of abuses.

With regard to doctrine, the council clarified the traditional teachings of the Catholic Faith. It affirmed that salvation is attained by both faith and good works. It stated also that the teachings of Christ are contained not only in the Bible but also in the living tradition of the Church. The legitimacy of all seven sacraments was upheld and the Mass was declared a true sacrifice. Moreover, the real presence of Our Lord in Communion was maintained. The council also affirmed certain other doctrines which Protestants had denied; such as the existence of purgatory, the value of the veneration of the saints, and the power of the Church to grant an indulgence.

With regard to discipline, a thorough reform was carried out. Bishops were made definitely subject to the Holy See, were required to reside in their dioceses, and to make regular inspections of the area under their jurisdiction to see that all was in order. No one was allowed to preach or hear confessions without the consent of the local bishop. Seminaries were to be established in each diocese and the qualifications for the priesthood were to be rigidly enforced. Members of religious orders were required to reside in their houses, to observe the rule of the order, and to wear clerical dress. Finally, certain abuses among the laity were touched on and the council required that all Catholics must be married before a priest and two witnesses.

Such were the reforms of the Council of Trent and, despite the fact that many rulers refused to allow them to be carried out immediately, the condition of the Church was vastly improved.

The Reform Continued. Even after the Council of Trent the papacy carried out other reforms. Pope Paul III revived the Roman Inquisition to root out heresy. In 1564 Pope Pius IV thoroughly revised the *Index of For-*

bidden Books, whose purpose was to protect the faithful from heretical writings. While mistakes occasionally were committed by these institutions, both served a useful purpose. Pope St. Pius V (1566-72) was also a great reformer. Under his leadership an official catechism was published so that all might have a ready guide to Catholic teaching. A revised missal appeared in 1570, and soon thereafter the clerical breviary was reformed. Finally, in 1604 a new version of the *Vulgate Bible* appeared.

The Reform Maintained. Reform had been carried out in the Church before, but often it had been allowed to lapse. Popes after Pius V were determined that this would not happen and down to 1648—the period covered by this chapter—they continued to maintain and extend the reform. Abuses were severely punished, the formation of seminaries was encouraged, and numerous new devotions, such as Forty Hours, were provided for the edification of the faithful.

In addition, the Church maintained its interest in art and learning. The new artistic style, the Baroque, was adopted and numerous churches and cathedrals were built. The magnificent Basilica of St. Peter was completed and the city of Rome was beautiful and improved. The greatest composer of the age, Pietro Luigi Palestrina, was encouraged to carry out a much needed reform of Church music. All in all, the continued sponsorship of art by the Church was a healthy contrast to most Protestants who fanatically banned all art and music from their churches.

Not only the papacy was active, however, for many bishops did much good. Foremost among them was St. Charles Borromeo. Named a cardinal at the age of twenty-two, very active at the Council of Trent, he eventually returned to the city of Milan to put the reform into operation. When he arrived there, the Church was in a bad state for it had not had a resident bishop

115

in some sixty years. St. Charles quickly took action. By establishing seminaries and personally visiting every parish in his diocese, he proved that the directives of the council could be carried out in a practical way.

New Religious Orders. The welfare of the Church was also improved by the work of the religious orders. The old orders—Benedictines, Franciscans, Dominicans, and others— were thoroughly reformed. In addition, numerous new orders appeared. The *Barnabites*, approved by the papacy in 1533, engaged in preaching and teaching. In 1540 St. Jerome Emilian secured approval for his order, the *Somaschi*, which made its main work the care of the poor. St. Angela Merici founded the *Ursulines*, an order of nuns which concentrated on the education of young girls.

More important than these was the work of St. Philip Neri (1515-95). His order, the *Oratorians*, was simply a free community of secular priests. No vows were taken and the members were free to return to the life of a secular priest at any time. Yet, they were of immense importance in leading souls back to God. Making use of music, group prayers, and a simple, direct style of preaching, the Oratorians were popular everywhere.

The most influential order of the period, however, was the *Society of Jesus*, or the Jesuits. Their founder, St. Ignatius Loyola, was a worldly, young Spanish soldier when an injury forced him into a hospital and brought about a personal commitment to Christ. Once recovered, he pursued an arduous course of education and at the University of Paris he found several like-minded companions. Taking private vows, they determined to undertake a mission to the Mohammedans, but when this became impossible they placed themselves at the disposal of the papacy.

Pope Paul III approved the order in 1540 and after that their growth was rapid. Requiring strict standards for admittance and long years of study before ordination, the order was built upon an almost military type of discipline. Each member was expected to render absolute obedience to his superior and a special vow of obedience to the pope was added to the three regular vows of poverty, chastity, and obedience. Soon Jesuits were to be found everywhere in Europe establishing educational institutions, advising rulers, and preaching the Gospel. Clearly, they were the most potent new weapon in the service of the Church.

The Revival of Catholic Theology was clearly needed to give the Church a strong intellectual foundation, but it was only partly achieved. Cardinal Cajetan (1469-1534) did a great deal to revive the theology of St. Thomas Aquinas and made contributions of his own. While other theologians appeared, no great theological works were produced. There were, however, numerous writings for the use of the laity. St. Peter Canisius (1521-93) was instrumental in the preparation of catechisms, and the *Spiritual Exercises* of St. Ignatius Loyola has remained the basis for most retreats to the present day.

Summary. Thus, through the work of numerous capable reformers the Church was stirred from her earlier lethargy and put in a position to once more properly carry out its true function. It was soon to make serious inroads on the great numbers lost to Protestantism.

The Wars of Religion

By the late sixteenth century the stage was set for a prolonged and bitter European struggle. The Protestants had had time to fully organize and the Church had completed its reform. The two were now ready to do battle for the loyalty of Europe, for it did not seem possible that both could continue to exist side by side. But before examining these wars, something must be said of the efforts of the Catholic Church to regain territories that had been lost to Protestantism.

The Counter-Reformation was the process by which

117

the Church, after reforming itself, sought to re-extend its spiritual authority throughout Europe. Missionary efforts played a large part in this movement. In Germany, the Jesuit, St. Peter Canisius was most active. By his constant work and preaching, in addition to his encouragement of Catholic princes, he probably saved half of Germany for the Faith. In Switzerland, St. Francis de Sales (1567-1622) preached everywhere and won thousands back from Calvinism.

In France, where the threat of Protestantism was very strong, St. Vincent de Paul (1580-1660) was in the forefront of the Catholic resurgence. His devoted service to the poor and destitute won respect everywhere. In addition, his influence was responsible for the formation of two important religious communities. The *Congregation of the Missions,* founded by St. Vincent in 1625, was active in preaching and gave numerous retreats for clergymen, greatly raising the standards of clerical life. Then, in 1632 St. Louise de Marillac, under the guidance of St. Vincent, founded the *Daughters of Charity,* the first order of nuns concentrating on work in the world. Even in England, there was a good deal of activity, for, despite persecution, great numbers of missionary priests risked, and often lost, their lives to keep the Faith alive.

But there was a second aspect to the Counter-Reformation. It involved the attempt on the part of certain Catholic princes to restore the Faith by force. And from this, and from similar attempts on the part of Protestant princes, came the Wars of Religion.

Philip II, king of Spain from 1556 to 1598, was the most determined Catholic champion during the last half of the sixteenth century. A strong ruler and the son of Emperor Charles V, he identified the welfare of the Church with the welfare of Spain. In 1517 he was instrumental in organizing a great naval fleet which defeated the Turks at the Battle of Lepanto and thus perhaps saved southern Europe. He then turned his attention to Protestantism, but despite vigorous efforts, he was largely unsuccessful. Unable to prevent the victory of Calvinism in Holland and that country's eventual independence from Spain, he then determined to restore England to the Faith. In 1588 he dispatched the great Armada to attack England, overthrow Elizabeth, and destroy Protestantism. But the famous "Protestant wind" threw the fleet into disarray and it was almost totally destroyed by the smaller, but more potent English ships.

The Struggle in France.   Philip also sought to intervene in France, although the issue there was largely out of his hands. In France the fate of religion became involved in an equally bitter struggle for political power. On the one side was the Guise family, strong defenders of Catholicism; on the other was the Bourbon family, the champion of the Huguenots, or French Protestants. In the middle, desperately trying to hold on to power, were three weak Valois kings, all guided by their unscrupulous mother, Catherine de Medici.

In 1572 Catherine, who was temporarily allied with the Guise family, perpetuated the infamous massacre of St. Bartholomew's day in which thousands of Huguenots were brutally killed. But their strength was not broken and civil war continued. Finally, with all other claimants dead, Henry Bourbon emerged the victor. When it became clear, however, that France would not accept a Protestant ruler, Henry converted to Catholicism, after supposedly declaring that "Paris is surely worth a Mass." Henry became one of France's greatest and most popular kings and in 1598 he issued the first real act of religious toleration—the *Edict of Nantes*—which granted the Huguenots the right to practice their religion and protected them from discrimination.

The Thirty Years War.   The last and most terrible of all the wars of religion occurred in Germany in the first half of the seventeenth century. All was religious chaos as Lutherans, Calvinists, and Catholics struggled for control of the country. Moreover, there was a political side to the struggle, for the German emperor was attempting to reimpose his power over the rebellious princes, many of whom were Protestant. Thus, the threat of war was always present. It finally came in 1618 when Bohemia, which was strongly Protestant, overthrew the Emperor Ferdinand and elected Count Frederick, the Protestant leader, in his place. Despite the strength of the princes and the determined help given to them by the Lutheran kings of Denmark and Sweden, the emperor was everywhere victorious and it seemed that German Protestantism was on its last legs. But then Catholic France, under the leadership of Cardinal Richelieu, joined the side of the princes to destroy the power of the emperor. The *Treaty of Westphalia* (1648) granted toleration to Calvinists, as well as Lutherans and Catholics, and the wars of religion had come to an end.

Summary. The year 1648 was thus an important turning point in the history of the Church. Catholicism, despite its vigorous reform had been unable to crush the Protestants. Moreover, the fact that Cardinal Richelieu used the power of Catholic France to destroy Catholic Germany, and that the protests of the pope against the Treaty of Westphalia were ignored, demonstrates that the interests of religion were being pushed aside in the interest of politics. The wars of religion proved little, except that Christians could kill each other, and the lesson did not greatly improve the image of the Faith.

Conclusion

The period from 1517 to 1648 was thus one of great difficulty for the Church. For the first time, its spiritual authority was successfully challenged in Europe. Seen from a missionary point of view, the Church had never before sustained such a loss. And yet the religion established by Christ carefully, but firmly, reformed its abuses while preserving the essentials of the Faith handed down by Christ and His Apostles. Thus, despite the revolt, the Church found itself stronger and better able to carry on its divine mission in 1648 than it had been in 1517.

But what is to be said of the Protestant Revolt? That it occurred is partially understandable because of the abuses in the Church. Moreover, it undoubtedly prompted the true reform carried out by the Church. But at the same time, no matter what were the intentions of the reformers themselves, it led countless individuals away from the consolation of the sacraments and the true teachings of Christ. Moreover, it brought about a serious split in the ranks of Christianity. Men, unable to agree on religious truth, were forced to push religion to the background and make it a purely private affair. The lamentable result was that the wisdom of Christianity slowly, but surely, lost its influence on society.

STUDY QUESTIONS

1. Distinguish the good from the bad in Luther's reform proposals.
2. What appealed to pious people of the sixteenth century in Luther's doctrine? What attracted people to Calvin's presentation of the message of Christ?
3. Contrast the Reformation in England with the Reformation in Germany.
4. How did Christ renew His disciples within the Body of the Church during the sixteenth century?
5. Describe how the procedure of the Fathers of the Council of Trent showed their consciousness of the presence of the Holy Spirit in the council.
6. It has been said that the opening of Vatican II closed

the Age of the Reformation. What does this mean? Why may it be true?

7. What events of the sixteenth century indicate that many members of the Church understood, but not very fully, the message of Christ?

8. What must the Christian world—Catholic and Protestant—of today keep in mind about the Reformation if the Ecumenical Movement is to be a success?

BIBLIOGRAPHY

BELLOC, HILAIRE. *Characters of the Reformation.* (Garden City, N.Y.: 1958).

(Contains short studies of most of the important figures in the English Reformation.)

DERLETH, AUGUST. *St. Ignatius and the Company of Jesus.* (New York: 1956).

(A good biography.)

DEWOHL, LOUIS. *The Golden Thread.* (Philadelphia: 1952).

(A popular life of St. Ignatius of Loyola.)

HOLLIS, CHRISTOPHER. *Thomas More.* (Milwaukee: 1934).

(A good biography of a great Catholic scholar who resisted with his life the English revolt against the Church.)

HUGHES, PHILIP. *A Popular History of the Reformation.* (Garden City, N.Y.: 1957).

(A good summary of the whole Reformation movement.)

MARCUSE, LUDWIG. *Soldier of the Church: The Life of Ignatius Loyola.* (New York: 1939).

(A good biography.)

MAYNARD, THEODORE. *Apostle of Charity.* (New York: 1939).

(A biography of St. Vincent de Paul.)

THOMPSON, EDWARD HEALY. *The Life of St. Charles Borromeo.* (London: 1893).

(A good biography of one of the great Catholic reformers.)

YEO, MARGARET. *Reformer: St. Charles Borromeo.* (Milwaukee· 1938).

(A good biography.)

Chapter **VI**

The Church
in an
Age of
Absolutism

CHRIST ABIDES WITH HIS PEOPLE

Introduction

THE Catholic Reformation produced a Church that was internally strong and vibrant. Abuses which had existed did not recur. Moreover, the Church took advantage of the great geographical discoveries of the period to significantly extend the boundaries of the Faith. But at the same time as the Church was expanding beyond Europe, its position in Europe was consistently weakened. Protestant rulers excluded the Church from their territories and Catholic rulers sought to control it. The thinkers of the age turned away from Christian truths, advocated an avid secularism, and undermined the influence of the Church. The result was the French Revolution which, before it was over, subjected Christianity to another bitter persecution.

123

The Expansion of the Missions

The Great Discoveries. The late fifteenth and early sixteenth centuries, which introduced so many other significant changes into the world, also witnessed what may be called a vast geographical explosion. Fired with the active spirit of the Renaissance, men determined to find new routes to the Orient, the source of trade and wealth. Portuguese efforts resulted in the voyage of Vasco da Gamma, who in 1498 reached India by sailing around Africa. Already, however, another more important discovery had been made. In 1492 Christopher Columbus, sailing under the flag of Spain, stumbled upon a vast new world in the Western Hemisphere. Soon, almost all Europe was engaged in a race for exploration and colonization. But more than this, these discoveries presented a great opportunity to the Church, which while undergoing the trials of the Reformation, had not forgotten the commandment of Christ to spread the Faith to all nations.

Papal Leadership. From the very beginning, the papacy had played an active and dominant role in the missionary work of the Church. It was only natural, then, that this trend continued. Most of the early missionary activity was carried on by religious orders and these, because of their international character, were more responsive to papal direction than the secular clergy. This may be especially noted in the work of the Jesuits who were tied closely to the papacy. Moreover, the papacy was in a position to better organize and direct missionary work. In 1622 Pope Gregory XV created the *Sacred Congregation for the Propagation of the Faith,* or as it is sometimes known, the Congregation of the Propaganda. It was responsible for the co-ordination of the Church's worldwide missionary activity, and while its directives were sometimes of disputed value, its work was of primary importance.

124

Africa. In the early days of the Church, North Africa had been Christian. But this was ended by the Mohammedan conquest, and missionary activity during the crusades was largely unsuccessful. The Portuguese explorations, however, opened up the possibility of missionary work among the natives of Central and Southern Africa, and in 1491 a Dominican mission went up the Congo River into the interior of the continent. At first successful, the difficulty of the terrain and Mohammedan pressure from the North prevented any significant success. Such, unfortunately, was the story with other African missions. The Jesuits, however, were temporarily successful in the African kingdom of Ethiopia, which followed a schismatic type of Christianity. In 1546 the Jesuits entered the region and for a while a reconciliation with Rome was achieved. But disagreements followed and real unity proved impossible. Africa, then, was little affected by missionary work; the evangelization of that continent awaited the nineteenth century.

Asia was the scene of greater success, for as soon as the Portuguese established colonies in the area, missionary activity was begun. Real success, however, started with the arrival of St. Francis Xavier in 1542. Working in the colony of Goa, his first task was to reform the Portuguese colonists, whose cruelty and scandalous lives did much to prevent conversions. Soon he extended his activity throughout southern India. Enjoying the gift of miracles, and making use of interpreters, he spoke to thousands of Indians and made numerous conversions. Moreover, he carefully instructed a few intelligent converts in each area to carry on the work. In 1549 St. Francis travelled to Japan where, after adopting the dress of a cultured Japanese, he secured from the emperor permission to preach. His labors resulted in conversions and the beginnings of Japanese Christianity. St. Francis then determined to work in China, the wealthiest and most influential of the Asian nations, but unfortunately he died in 1552 without reaching the mainland. In ten short years of work, however, he had laid the basis and formulated the techniques for an extensive missionary campaign throughout the East.

In India the work of St. Francis was carried on for some years, but success was achieved only among the lower classes. This situation changed with the arrival of Father Robert Nobili in 1608. Accepting the dress and customs of the Brahmin class, he made much progress among the upper classes. Moreover, he wisely allowed his Indian converts to retain any of their former customs that did not conflict with the Faith. Denounced to the papacy for supposed blending of pagan customs with Christian teaching, he was upheld by Pope Gregory XV. As a result, he and his associates won some 100,000 converts. But disputes continued concerning the retention of Indian customs and these disputes, in addition to the growing power of the Protestant Dutch and English in India, curbed further success.

In Japan Fathers Torres and Gago continued the work begun by St. Francis. Their success was great, for in 1585 it was reported to Rome that there were over 150,000 converts and some 200 chapels in the country. Unfortunately, however, the government turned against the work in 1587 and ordered all missionaries out of the country.

In China some success was achieved under Father Matteo Ricci who arrived in 1581. Dressing as a Mandarin, or Chinese scholar, and making great use of his scientific knowledge, he converted several influential Chinese. The Faith soon spread and, despite occasional government interference and disputes over the retention of Chinese customs, some 300,000 converts were won.

Latin America, except for the territory of Brazil, was

under the control of Spain and while the Spaniards were primarily interested in wealth, they nonetheless encouraged missionary activity. Missionaries followed Cortez into Mexico in 1519 and Pizarro into Peru in 1531. Eventually, Dominicans, Franciscans, Jesuits, and Spanish secular priests spread their activity throughout the whole continent. Conversions everywhere were numerous, and the total number of baptisms was in the millions. The apparition of the Blessed Mother to a Mexican native in 1513 at Guadalupe was a great aid in the evangelization of that country. The American Church also produced saints such as St. Rose of Lima (1586-1617), the first American to be canonized.

This success was achieved against great odds: the difficulties of working in an unknown geographical environment, and the constant interference of the Spanish government. The missionaries also did much to improve the lot of the natives with whom they came in contact. Constantly seeking to soften the cruelty of the Spanish colonists, they established villages to protect the natives from exploitation. Everywhere the Indians were instructed in crafts and trades. Even cultural life was not neglected, for many schools and unversities were established.

North America. Much less success was achieved north of the Rio Grande. The Indians were less civilized than their counterparts in the south and this made conversion difficult. Yet much was done. In the area of California, Father Serra began the establishment of his famous mission system in 1769, and over 50,000 Indians were baptized. In the southwest, missionaries, such as Father Kino, built churches and made many converts.

In *French North America* missionaries arrived in Canada as early as 1615. But the Indians were warlike, and there was little support from the French government. The Jesuits were very active, however, and produced such figures as the explorer Father Marquette and the martyr St. Isaac Jogues. By 1659 the city of Quebec received its own bishop. The French also spread the Faith through the Mississippi valley as far south as the port of New Orleans.

In the *Thirteen English Colonies* along the Atlantic seaboard, Catholics were generally unwelcome, for among the Protestant colonies only the Quakers of Pennsylvania allowed any real religious toleration. In the Catholic colony of Maryland, however, true religious toleration existed until Protestants took over control of the area. But by the time of the American Revolution there were only 25,000 Catholics and some 25 priests in all the colonies.

Summary. The missionary efforts of the early modern age not only achieved great success, they also prepared the way for future endeavors. For one thing, the missionaries learned of the danger of identifying the Faith with European culture, for it is not necessary to turn an Asian into a European in order to make a Christian of him. The non-European must be allowed to maintain whatever customs and traditions that do not conflict with the Faith. Moreover, the need for a native clergy was made clear. The refusal of the Spanish government to allow the ordination of Indians was a serious handicap to the welfare of the South American Church. It was a mistake not to be repeated. Finally, the success of the missions revealed the vitality and the strength of Christ's Church. A Faith, violently attacked in its European homeland, was finding new adherents across the seas.

The Church and the Absolute State

The power of the national states, which can be traced to the Age of Transition, continued to increase after the Reformation. Indeed, the Reformation promoted the growth of this power. By destroying European religious unity, it fostered nationalism and most of the new religions were organized along national lines. The Thirty Years War, with the defeat and destruction of the old empire, marked the victory of the national state. This victory, however, meant difficulty for the Church, because the new monarchs were as jealous of their power as Philip the Fair had been of his.

Gallicanism arose as a religious manifestation of the power of the national states. As a doctrine it held that both the political and spiritual authority of the papacy was limited by the will of the king. Quite naturally this idea was most vigorously followed in seventeenth-century France, the most powerful of the national states. As early as 1549 Pierre Pithou declared in *The Liberties of the French Church* that the king enjoyed extensive powers over the Church in France. As the French kings increased their power, due to the work of such men as Richelieu and Mazarin, the idea gained more and more approval, and even many churchmen accepted it.

The Regale Affair. When Louis XIV became king of France in 1660 the power of the French monarchy was at its height. Louis, moreover, was a man who knew his power. Constantly flattered and known as the "Sun king" he was not inclined to bow before anyone, even the pope. Thus, while Louis was a sincere Catholic in his beliefs, trouble was to be expected. In 1662 a fight broke out between French guards and the papal guard in Rome. Although the French were probably at fault, Louis blustered to such an extent that Pope Alexander VII (1655-67) was forced to apologize. More serious trouble followed in 1673. The French kings had long possessed a privilege known as the *régale,* which allowed them to receive the revenues from certain French bishoprics when they were vacant, and to appoint all diocesan clergy during the vacancy. In 1673 the king, solely on his own authority, extended this privilege to all of France. Two bishops immediately appealed to Rome against this usurpation and Pope Innocent XI (1676-89) upheld them, denying the king's right to take such an action. A long conflict was in the offing.

The Gallican Articles. Louis eventually retaliated against the papacy. Knowing that some French bishops were on his side and that others could be forced into line, he convoked an Assembly of the French Church in 1682. Under the leadership of Bishop Bossuet, Louis' ecclesiastical right-hand man, the assembly passed the famous four *Gallican Articles.* They declared that: 1) the pope has no political power over kings, 2) the power of the papacy is limited by a general council, 3) the papacy must respect the "liberties" of the French Church, and 4) the ruling of the pope on a matter of dogma is not infallible unless accepted by the whole Church. The articles, therefore, questioned not only the political, but also the spiritual power of the papacy. Louis directed, moreover, that the articles should be taught in all French seminaries. Innocent XI immediately condemned the articles and to enforce his point of view refused to confirm any of the king's appointments of bishops. As the number of vacancies grew, Louis was apparently faced with the alternative of taking the French Church into schism or submitting. But wishing to do neither, he contented himself with intimidating the pope by confiscating papal property.

The Settlement. The next pope, Alexander VIII (1689-91), was anxious to avoid a split and made a few concessions, but he continued to condemn the Gallican Articles. The way for a solution was, however, prepared. Pope Innocent XII (1691-1700) finally ended the long quarrel. In 1693 a compromise was reached when Louis withdrew the Gallican Articles and the pope, in turn, confirmed his appointments. The papacy had not achieved a total victory, however. The king still controlled ecclesiastical appointments, and the Gallican Articles continued to be taught. Even worse was the fact that Gallican ideas spread to other Catholic countries. The eighteenth century was to see the revival of Gallicanism under another name and in another country.

Febronianism was the eighteenth century version of Gallicanism in Germany. A German bishop, Johann von Hontheim, writing under the name "Febronius," published a book in which he clearly denied the spiritual power of the papacy. Claiming that all bishops were equal in their power and that only a general council had ultimate authority, he called on secular rulers to aid in the restriction of papal rule. Pope Clement XIII (1758-69) condemned the book in 1764 and Febronius submitted to the condemnation twelve years later. Other German bishops nonetheless took up his ideas and in 1786 they demanded episcopal freedom from Rome. Forced themselves to yield, they soon found their demands furthered by the Austrian emperor.

Josephinism is the name given to the ecclesiastical policy of the Austrian emperor, Joseph II (1765-90). A reformer, he was anxious to change old customs and some good was achieved, but unfortunately he considered the Church as simply a department of state and did not hesitate to interfere in purely religious questions. Declaring that bishops were not responsible to Rome, he went on to direct that no papal orders were valid in Austria without the consent of the emperor. In addition, he removed clerical control from education and suppressed all religious orders.

Even the liturgy was not free from Joseph's interference, for he went so far as to change the number of holydays and to prescribe the number of candles to be used on the altars. Pope Pius VI (1775-99) journeyed to Vienna in 1782 to persuade the emperor to change his ways, but achieved no real success. Joseph died in 1790, however,

131

and his successor reversed much of his legislation. But the threat of a state controlled Church was not ended, for Pius VI was to live to see the French Revolution and to discover that the extinction of kings did not necessarily promote the freedom of the Church.

The Threat of Heresy

In addition to those of the Protestant Reformation, the Church was challenged by new heresies in the seventeenth and eighteenth centuries. The two most important of these were *Jansenism* and *Quietism*.

Jansenism arose from the ideas of a certain Cornelius Jansen (1585-1638). The Council of Trent had declared that man was saved both by the grace of God and man's co-operation by the performance of good works. But disputes broke out concerning the relative importance of grace and works. They became so bitter that the papacy was forced to impose silence on the warring factions in 1606. Jansen, however, was anxious to find a solution to the problem, and in order to do so he went back to the writings of St. Augustine.

Unfortunately, he misunderstood Augustine's doctrine and came to the position that original sin made it impossible for man to do good. Thus, man could be saved only by the grace of God, which is not given to everyone. Jansen's theory was, therefore, very close to predestination and it has often been called "Calvinism in the Catholic Church." Jansen died in 1638, but his book, the *Augustinus*, was published by friends in 1640. Under the leadership of two men, St. Cyran and Antoine Arnauld, its ideas began to spread and one of Arnauld's sisters, Angelique, established the headquarters of the Jansenist movement at the Convent of Port Royal where she was the mother superior.

The Dispute over Communion. Jansen's ideas on grace and salvation were too difficult to affect ordinary people,

132

but this situation was changed in 1643 when Antoine Arnauld published *On Frequent Communion*. In this book he insisted that Communion should be received only very seldom since no one is worthy to receive it. Rather than considering Communion as a supernatural aid to leading a good life, he looked upon it as a reward. Arguing that perfect contrition was necessary for absolution, he advocated a morality that was unduly strict. The Jesuits, who had been encouraging the frequent reception of Communion, leaped to the attack and, with the co-operation of St. Vincent de Paul and Sorbonne University, drew up a list of five propositions held by the Jansenists. These were sent to the papacy and in 1653 Pope Innocent X condemned the propositions as heretical. But the matter was not so easily settled.

Jansenist Hedging. To escape condemnation, the Jansenists now hit upon a ruse. They agreed that the five propositions had been rightly condemned, but they denied that Jansen had ever held such ideas. The papacy replied in 1656. Pope Alexander VII declared that the five propositions were contained in the writings of Jansen. But the Jansenists, including four bishops, continued to resist and not until 1669 did they half-heartedly submit.

Jansenism's Last Round. In 1671, however, Pasquier Quesnel revived Jansenist ideas in his *Moral Reflections on the New Testament*. When this was condemned in 1708 there was again resistance. Finally, in 1713 Pope Clement XI issued the bull *Unigenitus* as a final condemnation of the heresy. But disputes followed regarding the enforcement of the bull. When it was learned that certain priests were refusing the last sacraments to suspected Jansenists, the French courts took action. The archbishop of Paris, for example, was forced into exile for using such measures. In 1756 Pope Boniface XIV ended the dispute

133

by once again condemning Jansenism, while directing that the last sacraments were to be refused only to unrepentant, notorious public sinners. The quarrel finally died down, although a few Jansenists went to the Netherlands and established a schismatic church.

Quietism, the other heresy of the age, came from the teachings of a Spanish priest, Michael Molinos (1627-96). Living in Rome as a spiritual adviser to a group of nuns, he published *A Spiritual Guide* in 1675. According to Molinos, one must be completely submissive to divine inspiration in order to lead a truly spiritual life. Prayer must consist solely of contemplation—listening to God— and is not to involve any positive activity. Even temptations are not to be resisted, since to do so would require a positive act of the will, instead of submissiveness to God, the possible source of the temptation. Thus, the doctrine of Molinos was a sort of mysticism run wild and when he and his group put it into practice, the result was a peculiar mixture of contemplation and immorality. Brought before the Inquisition in 1685, Molinos was found guilty of heresy and in 1688 Pope Innocent XI condemned his teaching.

Quietism in France. The ideas of Molinos were nonetheless taken up by Madame Guyon, a young French widow seeking religious satisfaction. This lady, with her spiritual adviser, went around France preaching a doctrine of "pure love" until arrested by the archbishop of Paris in 1687. She was soon released, however, and became a spiritual adviser at St. Cyr, a fashionable girls' school maintained by the crown. At this point, Bossuet secured the condemnation of her ideas. Madame Guyon submitted in 1696 but was subsequently defended by Bishop Fénelon, who felt that she was being persecuted. A long quarrel followed between Bossuet and Fénelon and did not end until the papacy condemned certain of Fénelon's statements. The latter, a sincere Christian, quickly submitted and the movement came to an end.

Summary. Neither Jansenism nor Quietism resulted in a wholesale desertion from the Church, but both had evil effects. Jansenism introduced a measure of puritanism into the Church which has been difficult to overcome. Moreover, the long dispute which it caused seriously weakened the unity of the French Church. Quietism, on the other hand, tended to discredit all spirituality. Its unfortunate excesses led many to suspect that all contemplation was somehow wrong.

The Church and the Enlightenment

Beginning with the Age of Transition, the Church had lost control of Europe's intellectual development. This divorce of sacred and profane knowledge was continued by the Renaissance and the work of the seventeenth century. The philosophy of that age cut itself off from divine revelation and based itself on reason alone. Moreover, the scientific advances of such men as Galileo and Newton demonstrated what reason could achieve and, in the process, badly embarrassed the Church, since many churchmen were shown to have held obviously incorrect opinions about the universe. The fact that Galileo had been condemned by the Inquisition for teaching that the earth revolved around the sun was not easily lived down. The confidence in reason gave birth, therefore, to an intellectual movement known as the Enlightenment.

The Nature of the Enlightenment. It would be impossible to fully describe the ideas of the Enlightenment in such a small space, but some indication can be given of its major ideas. In the first place, the Enlightenment advocated *rationalism.* Everything was to be subjected to man's reason and whatever could not be proved solely from reason was to be rejected. In one blow, therefore, the Enlightenment denied divine revelation since it was not subject to rational confirmation.

The Enlightenment also fostered *naturalism.* Man was advised to conform himself to nature and the natural law;

135

but this natural law was to be discovered by reason alone. Thus, the Enlightenment was anti-traditional. All authority and all tradition were to be rejected unless they could be shown to conform to nature. The method idolized by the Enlightenment was the method of science. The seeking of religious truth was rejected as a waste of time, and the scientific study of the "real" world was deemed more important. The Enlightenment was also extremely secularistic. Based on vague ideas of humanitarianism, it believed that it could create a better world for all by education and a process of social engineering. All those agencies which restricted human "progress," such as the Church, were to be overthrown. Finally, the Enlightenment rejected all the privileges of the nobility and the Church, and called for a state in which the middle class would rule, with the aid of a co-operative monarch if possible, but without him if necessary. Many of the ideas of the Enlightenment were, therefore, highly subversive of religion.

Deism was the basic religious doctrine of the Enlightenment. Its desire was to find a natural religion to which all men could subscribe. This religion was to be based on reason, not "superstition," and was to avoid as much dogma as possible. Basically, Deism accepted a God, but this God was a sort of divine clockmaker who having created and wound up the clockwork of the universe allowed it to run on without interference. It was a God who would not "upset" the regularity of nature by performing miracles; it was a God who would not bother with revelation, since all could be learned from nature; and it was certainly not a God who would become man, for Christ was nothing more than a pious, perhaps misled, moral reformer. In short, it was not a Christian God.

Important figures of the Enlightenment, therefore, were all anti-Catholic. Francis Arouet (1694-1778), known as Voltaire, used his extremely clear and witty mind to heap ridicule on Church and nobility alike. Denis Diderot (1713-84) edited the famous *Encyclopédie* whose treatment of religion and Christianity was highly critical. Jean Jacques Rousseau (1712-78) denied the existence of original sin and called for a radical democratic government based on a deistic religion.

The Freemasons became one of the chief agencies by which the ideas of the Enlightenment were spread. The movement began in 1717 in England and soon spread to the continent of Europe. The *Masonic Order* was a secret society with all the customary rites and ceremonies. Its religious ideas were deistic and certain of the more radical lodges engaged in anti-Catholic, and even anti-Christian, practices. In 1738 Pope Clement XII condemned the order and forbade any Catholic to belong to it, but this restriction was taken lightly by many Catholics, and not a few members of the clergy. The many charges of plots and conspiracies made against the Masons are perhaps exaggerated, but there can be no doubt that they and other similar groups, were of immense importance in spreading the dangerous ideas of the Enlightenment among the educated middle class.

The Suppression of the Jesuits was one lamentable result of the anti-Catholicism of the late eighteenth century. The Jesuits unfortunately had made a great number of enemies. Many kings, and all those who shared Gallican ideas, denounced the unswerving loyalty of the Jesuits to the Holy See. Other religious orders, and some bishops, resented their influence in the Church. The Jansenists kindled an undying hatred for the Jesuits because of their opposition to Jansenist heresy.

Those who were anti-Catholic determined to destroy the Jesuits, since they were the most powerful and influential supporters of the Church. In the minds of many, the fall of the Society of Jesus would be the first step in the complete destruction of the Faith. But the Jesuits were no easy target. The Society had some 25,000 mem-

137

bers, they controlled great numbers of colleges and universities, and they were often the advisers of kings. Moreover, they had always been fervently protected by the papacy.

In the late eighteenth century, however, the enemies of the Society combined to overthrow them. The process began in Portugal where the prime minister, Pombal, accused the Society of taking part in a plot to murder the king. Thus in 1759 all Jesuits in the country were either imprisoned or exiled. The process was much the same in France, where a Jansenist controlled court made use of a legal case against the Jesuits to order the suppression of the Society. Similar action followed in Spain and most of the other Catholic countries.

Finally, pressure was brought on the papacy to disband the order altogether. Pope Clement XIII (1758-69) refused to take action and protected the Society, but his death opened the floodgates. The election of a new pope was delayed by the European powers anxious to obtain a more "co-operative" pontiff and their demands were finally met with the election of Clement XIV (1769-74). A weak man, anxious to antagonize no one, he issued the bull *Dominus Ac Redemptor* which suppressed the Society of Jesus. No charges were made against the order, but it was disbanded, the pope announced, for the peace of the Church. It was, however, a terrible blow. In an age when the Faith was attacked from every side, the Church had lost its most determined defender, and the missions were dealt a loss which could not wholly be repaired, despite the efforts of other orders.

The Church and the French Revolution

For a long time a steam had been brewing in Europe. A resentment of abuses and outworn privileges combined with the idea of the Enlightenment produced a truly volatile situation. The explosion finally broke forth in France. In 1789 Louis XVI, in desperate need of money,

138

called the meeting of the Estates-General. Controlled by the middle class, the Third Estate declared itself the National Assembly of France, did away with feudalism and all privileges, and drew up a constitution creating a limited monarchy. Moreover, the position of the Church was soon threatened by the revolution, for the Church had been a privileged institution in France and many of the leaders of the revolution were determined followers of Enlightened thought.

The Preliminary Phase. The revolutionary government of France soon found itself short of money. Thus, on October 10, 1789, Bishop Talleyrand suggested that the assembly should confiscate the property of the Church. After hot debate this was passed on November 2, 1789. The suppression of all religious orders quickly followed. Since the confiscation of Church property left the secular clergy without any financial support, the assembly took a further and more significant step. The king had previously controlled the Church; the assembly would now do likewise.

The result was the *Civil Constitution of the Clergy* passed on July 12, 1790. The provisions of this act were: 1) The number of dioceses were reduced to correspond with the political organization of the country. Bishops were henceforth to be elected by democratic assemblies, and the pope was merely to be notified of the choice. 2) Parishes were similarly reorganized and parish priests were also to be elected. 3) The salaries of the clergy were set; those of the hierarchy were lowered, and those of the lower clergy were raised. It was hardly to be expected, however, that the papacy could accept such legislation, and on April 13, 1791, Pope Pius VI condemned the Civil Constitution. But despite this, the assembly required all French clergymen to take an oath to observe the Civil Constitution. Some did so, but most refused and these were immediately subjected to persecution.

The Attack on Christianity. As the revolution progressed, it became more and more radical. The coming of the Jacobins to power in 1793 resulted in a "reign of terror" and a determined attack on the Faith. A new calendar was prepared to efface the memory of Christian holydays, education was removed from clerical control, and priests who refused to take the oath to the Civil Constitution were placed under sentence of death. There were even attempts to institute new religions. The Cathedral of Norte Dame witnessed the spectacle of a dancing girl adorned as the "goddess of reason" and worshipped on the high altar. Next followed Robespierre's "cult of the Supreme Being." The revolutionaries had turned from the worship of God to the worship of the revolution. But most of France remained Catholic, at least in sympathy, and the new religions were never popular. The overthrow of Robespierre, the Jacobin "high priest," in July of 1794 ended the most serious persecution of the Church.

A period of confusion followed. The new government, the Directory, persecuted or tolerated depending upon what group was in power. Meanwhile, the papacy demonstrated that it was not opposed to democracy in principle, for in June, 1796, Pius VI ordered French Catholics to obey all just legislation of the Republic. France, however, was by now at war with most of Europe and in 1796 the French armies invaded the Papal States. In 1797 Napoleon forced a humiliating treaty on the pope. This was soon followed by a French engineered revolt in Rome and the establishment of a Roman Republic. Pius VI, old and sick, was imprisoned and brought to France where he died on August 29, 1799. To many it seemed that the final destruction of the Church was imminent and some predicted that the cardinals would not bother to elect a new pope.

The Recovery of the Church. But Pius VI was not the last pope. In November of 1799 the cardinals were finally able to meet in Venice where they elected Gregorio Chiaramonte as Pius VII (1799-1823). It was an excellent choice, for the new pope knew how to be either tough or conciliatory as the occasion demanded. Moreover, he acquired an excellent adviser in Cardinal Consalvi, his Secretary of State and one of the last lay cardinals. Meanwhile, things had changed in France. Napoleon, having seized power, was now in full command and while he was not a religious man, he was a realist. Determined to restore order to the country, he knew that religious peace demanded the restoration of Catholicism, the religion of the great majority of the people.

The Concordat of 1801. Napoleon soon approached the papacy, and after long negotiations with Cardinal Consalvi the Concordat was signed. Its major provisions were as follows: 1) Catholicism was declared the religion of the majority of the French people, but other sects were to be tolerated. 2) The Church was not to recover its confiscated property, but the state was to provide for clerical salaries. 3) Bishops were to be nominated by Napoleon, but confirmed by the pope. Thus, the Catholic religion was restored to France. Napoleon, however, immediately pulled a doublecross and issued the *Organic Articles* which had the effect of subjecting the Church to state control.

Conflict between Empire and Papacy inevitably followed as Napoleon's ambition and power grew. When Pius VII came to Paris in 1804 to preside at Napoleon's coronation as emperor, a split was already evident. Napoleon's disregard of the rights of the Church in conquered Germany and Italy led to bitter feelings, as did the pope's refusal to grant a divorce to one of the emperor's brothers. A final break occurred when the pope refused to enforce the emperor's ban on English imports into the Papal States.

In 1808 the French again seized Rome, and in 1809 the

Papal States were made part of the French Empire. In that same year the pope was arrested and eventually brought to France. Pius replied by excommunicating those responsible for his capture and by refusing to confirm any of Napoleon's episcopal appointments. Moreover, the French bishops did not prove as easy to handle as Napoleon had anticipated. Military difficulties further hurt the position of the emperor. The earlier victories degenerated into the defeat in Russia and this was followed by the even more disastrous Battle of Nations in 1813. In 1814 Napoleon was forced to abdicate and the pope was allowed to return to Rome. Pius VII had thus successfully defied the most powerful man in Europe. Moreover, he proved himself a true Christian by his actions in behalf of his fallen opponent. When Napoleon was exiled to the island of St. Helena after his final defeat at Waterloo in 1815, Pius wrote asking that he be treated leniently. Apparently moved by a strange respect for his fallen persecutor, the pope went on to excuse Napoleon's errors and to praise him for the restoration of the Church to France. Pius had the satisfaction of learning that the emperor died, apparently having received the last sacraments of the Church.

Religious Life in the Age of Absolution

The liturgy underwent no significant changes in these centuries. But an important new devotion was introduced: that of the Sacred Heart of Jesus. In 1674 Our Lord appeared to St. Margaret Mary Alacoque, who was primarily responsible for popularizing the devotion. With its stress on the great love of Christ for humanity, it was an excellent corrective to the cold rationalism of the day.

Christian thought was severely hampered by the intellectual currents of the time. The doctrine of St. Thomas Aquinas was again in decline and no significant works in doctrinal theology were produced. But great advances were made in moral theology, primarily due to the work of St. Alphonsus Liguori (1691-1787). His principles of morality showed a healthy moderation and happily contradicted the strictness of Jansenism.

New religious orders were also formed during the period. The *Passionists*, organized by St. Paul of the Cross (1694-1775), combined a rigorous monastic life with active preaching. St. Alphonsus Liguori founded the *Redemptorists* who were especially active in preaching and in combating the enemies of the Church. Finally, the *Christian Brothers* were brought into existence by St. John Baptist de La Salle (1651-1719). An order of lay brothers, it was especially active in the education of young men.

Conclusion

When someone once asked a French politician what he had done during the French Revolution, his answer was, "I survived." Well might the Church give such an answer if it were asked what it had done during the Age of Absolutism. Survival in the face of heretics, ambitious rulers, secularist thinkers, and the ravages of the French Revolution was no easy matter. Indeed, had it not been for the divine institution of the Church it probably would not have survived. But, in truth, the Church did more than survive. The trials in Europe were balanced by the immense success of the Church in the extension of the Faith. These missionary accomplishments were the great glory of the Church in the Age of Absolutism.

STUDY QUESTIONS

1. Why is "Christ Abides with His People" a fitting subtitle for the history of the Church in the Age of Absolutism?
2. What is the best proof of the success of the Catholic Reformation of the previous century? Why?

3. In what way have some Catholic kings misunderstood the message of Christ?
4. Are there any remains of the heresy of Jansenism in the world today? Describe them.
5. Why did the Church lose the loyalty of so many well educated people in this period of her history?
6. Why didn't the Church come to an end in 1799? Why would anyone think that it would have come to an end in 1799?
7. How does one explain the anti-clericalism of the French Revolution?
8. Compare the opportunity for apostolic action by Christians today with the opportunity for apostolic action in the Age of Absolutism.

BIBLIOGRAPHY

CULLEN, THOMAS FRANCIS. *The Spirit of Serra.* (New York: 1935).
(A good biography of the man who established the famous California mission system.)

DUTTO, LOUIS ANTHONY. *The Life of Bartolome de Las Casas.* (St. Louis: 1902).
(A good treatment of the Spanish missionary work in South America.)

GOYAU, GEORGES. *Missions and Missionaries.* (London: 1932).
(A good study of Catholic missionary activity.)

McGRATTY, ARTHUR R. *The Fire of Francis Xavier.* (Milwaukee: 1952).
(A good biography of the most spectacular of all the Catholic missionaries.)

NEILL, THOMAS P. *Makers of the Modern Mind.* (Milwaukee: 1949).
(Contains good treatments of the most important formulators of modern thought.)

SARGENT, DANIEL. *Catherine Tekakwitha.* (New York: 1936).
(Good for an account of the French missionary work in Canada.)

Chapter **VII**

The Church
in the
Nineteenth
Century

THE BODY OF CHRIST COMES
TO NEW STRENGTH

Introduction

S INCE the Age of Transition the Church was constantly
attacked by an increasingly secular world. The end
of the French Revolution and the overthrow of Napoleon,
however, seemed to promise some relief for the Faith.
The post revolutionary age was tired of disorder and
yearned to turn back the clock in the hope of restoring
the more peaceful days of the past. But this yearning for
the past proved only a temporary thing, for the ideas of
the French Revolution—both good and bad—did not die
and could not be killed. Thus, after a short respite, the
temporal and spiritual authority of the Church was attacked from every side. But the Church of the nineteenth
century grew strong in the face of these attacks. Under
the leadership of extremely capable popes, it produced
numerous saints and religious orders, encouraged the re-

145

vival of missionary work, and saw the rise of a strong Catholicism in the United States.

The World of the Nineteenth Century

The story of the Church in the nineteenth century is extremely complex and is almost impossible to understand without some knowledge of the major forces in the life of the time. For that reason, it is necessary to briefly note some of the major trends of the age.

The Return of the Old Regime. The thinkers of the Enlightenment had promised that man would be able to build a better world by the use of his unaided reason. But the French Revolution had not produced this world, and consequently there was a temporary reaction to the ideas of the revolution. The old rulers—kings and nobles —returned, and people prepared to give them another chance. At the same time, the intellectual movement of the early nineteenth century—*romanticism*—rejected many of the ideas of the Enlightenment. Emotion was preferred to reason and men were advised to replace doubt with belief. Old traditions and institutions were to be respected rather than overthrown.

But a return to the past could not endure. The kings soon proved themselves unfit to rule and the middle class determined to regain control. A long series of revolutions throughout Europe eventually brought this about and as a result, many ideas from the Enlightenment and the French Revolution returned. It would be well to examine some of these ideas.

Liberalism was one of the major trends. Difficult to describe, it was the most important doctrine in the arsenal of the middle class. Much of it was good, as for example, the liberal demand for freedom of press, speech, and religion. But often it went too far. In their anxiety for freedom, liberals tended to deny all authority, and

146

especially the authority of the Church. Even worse, liberalism was generally secularistic. It wanted to drive religion from any place in the state and to make it a purely private affair. Thus, it constantly attacked both Church and clergy.

Nationalism was the great product of the French Revolution. It may be defined as a sort of patriotism run wild. As such it is the highest manifestation of the power of the national state, for it declares that man's highest loyalty is to his country. The Church has always taught that patriotism is a good thing, but it is a perversion to hold that loyalty to one's country is even higher than one's adherence to the moral law and the teachings of Christ. Nationalism was dangerous for another reason. Italians and Germans were anxious to unify their countries, and in Italy such a development meant the extinction of the temporal power of the papacy.

Materialism was another important trend of the age. It was of two kinds. Practical materialism involved a complete concern with the affairs of this life and a neglect of supernatural things. Partly the result of the Industrial Revolution which made the "good life" more possible than ever before, practical materialism made material progress the subject of its worship. An overbearing concern with business and industry relegated religion to a secondary and even unimportant place in the lives of many men.

Theoretical materialism was involved in the great scientific discoveries of the age. Men came to believe that the universe could be explained solely by material causes and the need for a creator was rejected. Thus, there was the rise of atheism.

Socialism arose to challenge many of the conditions of the middle class world. The lower classes, deprived of political rights and forced to work in terrible conditions for absurdly low wages, were dissatisfied. Many of them turned, therefore, to the doctrines of such socialists as Karl Marx, the founder of Communism. Marx correctly analyzed the injustices of nineteenth century life, but his solution was no better. Because some used religion to keep the workers in line—by telling them that they need not worry about terrible conditions since life was short and heaven would soon be theirs—Marx rejected religion altogether. Instead, he advised the workers to violently revolt, cast off the rule of the middle class, and build their own brand of earthly "paradise."

Thus, most of the trends of the age took an anti-Christian direction and were therefore dangerous for the Church.

The Catholic Revival in the Early Nineteenth Century

Although the Church had been violently attacked during the French Revolution, the overthrow of Napoleon brought a revival of sympathy for the Faith. The perseverance of Pius VII brought much respect to the papacy. The Church determined to reassert its place in the world and this determination was aptly demonstrated by the fact that Pius VII restored the Society of Jesus in 1814.

The Diplomacy of the Church. After the defeat of Napoleon, the leading statesmen of Europe gathered at the Congress of Vienna to reconstruct Europe. The pope's representative, Cardinal Consalvi, was also there and he made use of his great talents to secure the restoration of almost all of the Papal States to the pope. Soon after, he began negotiations with most of the European countries in order to redefine the status of the Church. As a result, concordats were signed with France, and most of the Catholic and Protestant states of Germany. While some of the states involved did not always observe the agreements, they were nonetheless favorable to the Church. The very fact that they were signed at all dealt a death blow to Gallicanism, for by signing such agreements the European rulers admitted, in effect, that the pope and not the king was the head of the Church.

The Popes and Italy. Due to the efforts of Cardinal Consalvi, the papacy had regained the Papal States. But there was great dispute about how these territories should be ruled. Some of the cardinals, called the *Zelanti,* favored a strict, conservative type of government. Others, the so called *Politiques,* advised a more lenient and progressive system. Pius VII and Consalvi endorsed the latter view. Many of the better reforms of the French Revolution were retained, a better administration was introduced, and such outmoded practices as the use of torture in legal proceedings were abolished.

But these reforms did not please those who wished to drive out the papacy altogether in order to make the Papal States part of a united Italy. The two popes after Pius VII, Leo XII (1823-29) and Pius VIII (1829-30), got through their reigns without serious trouble. But Gregory XVI (1831-46) was faced with a revolt in the first year of his reign, and the help of Austrian troops was needed to put it down. Gregory spent the rest of his pontificate attempting to repress revolutionary tendencies. But these continued to boil just under the surface and his successor was to experience even greater difficulty.

The Catholic Revival in France. The French Revolution had tried, but it had not succeeded in destroying the French Church. If anything, Catholicism was stronger after the revolution than it had been before. The Bourbon kings, who returned to govern the country, defended the Church, although they often sought to control it as well. Nonetheless they agreed to a concordat which contained the best features of the one Napoleon had signed in 1801. The Church was thus left free to carry on its work. At the same time, France produced numerous thinkers who defended the Faith and simultaneously

149

attacked the doctrines of the Enlightenment. Foremost among these was François Chateaubriand. His *Genius of Christianity* attempted to show civilization's need for the Faith. Unfortunately, however, he tended to extol Christianity because it was beautiful, and often forgot the sounder intellectual basis for belief.

In 1830 the situation in France changed when the middle class overthrew the Bourbon king, Charles X, and replaced him with a more "liberal" claimant, Louis Philippe. The new government was not overly unfavorable to the Church, but, it raised the delicate question of whether or not Catholics could support a regime which accepted some of the principles of the French Revolution. Most Catholics hesitated to do so, but a small group of men urged that the Church must make its peace with the modern world and accept a government based on the people. The leader of this group, Félicité de Lamennais, argued that the old monarchical governments had always dominated the Church and therefore that the Church should take its side with the people. Calling for political liberty and freedom of the press and speech, he and his associates founded a newspaper, *The Future,* with the motto: "God and Liberty."

When Lamennais and his group were attacked by the French hierarchy, they determined to go to Rome for approval. This was not given, however, because Gregory XVI was essentially a conservative and because Lamennais had gone too far on several points. Eventually the pope condemned certain of Lamennais' teachings in the bull, *Mirari Vos.* As a result, the proud Lamennais left the Church. But two of his associates, Lacordaire and Montalembert, remained in the Church and did much to show that many of the ideas of the modern world could be reconciled with the Faith.

The Church in Germany also experienced a revival in the early nineteenth century. The concordats provided the Church with needed freedom from the old ideas of

Febronianism and Josephinism and many influential converts were won. Typical of these was Joseph Goerres, a brilliant and fearless writer, who did much to win a favorable audience for the Faith among intellectuals.

One serious problem arose, however, in the Protestant state of Prussia. This state had a large Catholic minority and in 1803 it passed a law that in the case of mixed marriages, children would be raised in the religion of the father. This, of course, violated Church law, but one of the leading German bishops supported the legislation and the papacy made what concessions it could. In 1835, however, the new Archbishop of Cologne, Clemens Augustus von Droste-Vischering, determined to uphold the Catholic position. As a result, the government **arrested** him in 1837. But when German Catholics resisted such injustice, the government was forced to back down: arrested bishops were released and the state stopped its interference in mixed marriages. The Church had won a significant victory.

The Church in England. Since the Reformation, the English Government had discriminated against Catholics in a number of ways: no Catholic could hold a government position, and worship had to be strictly private. In the early nineteenth century, however, this situation changed. Fear of growing resistance in Catholic Ireland, added to an increasing respect for the papacy due to the resistance of Pius VII to Napoleon, forced Parliament to make changes. In 1829 the great Irish leader, Daniel O'Connell, and his "Catholic Association" secured the passage of a Catholic Emancipation Act. By its terms, Catholics were allowed to vote, sit in Parliament, and worship in their own churches.

Shortly thereafter, the Church made a few notable English converts. The "Oxford Movement" which began as an attempt to purify the dogmas and rituals of the Anglican Church, eventually led many to the true Faith.

151

Foremost among these was John Henry Newman, a great theologian, and later a cardinal. The Catholic Church did not, of course, become the dominant Faith in England, but the fact that the Church was given its freedom marked a significant achievement.

Pius IX and the Mid-Century Challenge

By the middle of the nineteenth century, the attempt to revive the old order had clearly broken down. The ideas of the French Revolution and the Enlightenment returned and the Church was bitterly attacked. Most of these attacks converged on one man. Pope Pius IX (1846-78), who enjoyed, or shall we say suffered, the longest reign of any modern pope.

The "Liberal" Pope. The election of Giovanni Mastai-Ferretti as Pius IX on June 16, 1846 brought wild rejoicing throughout Italy. Pius had criticized the conservative policies of his predecessors and had the reputation of being a liberal. Much was expected of him and he soon set out to effect his program in the Papal States. Political prisoners were released, restrictions on the press were lessened, a general reform of the laws was carried out, and such progressive things as railroads and street lights were introduced. Pius even went so far as to grant laymen a role in the government of the Papal States and in 1848 he issued a constitution which in effect made the pope a limited monarch insofar as his temporal power was concerned. Everywhere, even in Protestant countries, Pius was hailed as a progressive ruler.

The Revolution. But no matter how "liberal" Pius proved to be, one problem could not be solved. Many Italians were demanding a united Italy which would include the Papal States. The Papal States, however, were the property of the Church and Pius could not surrender them. In 1848 a revolution broke out in Italy and soldiers from all over the peninsula gathered to drive out the Austrian armies in the north. Pius, however, refused to allow the papal troops to participate because, he argued, the pope was the head of all Catholics and could not take the side of one country against another in a purely political matter. The Italian liberals were infuriated at this decision and a revolt in Rome was the outcome. The pope's prime-minister was murdered and Pius himself was forced to flee the city in disguise. A Roman Republic was established and it was not until 1849 that French troops were able to put down the revolutionary government. In July of 1849, Pius IX returned to Rome a changed man. His liberalism had apparently betrayed him and he determined henceforth to follow a conservative policy.

The Loss of the Papal States. Despite the failure of 1848 Italy did achieve unification. The kingdom of Piedmont-Sardinia, under the leadership of its brilliant but anti-clerical prime minister, Count Cavour, brought about this unification by force. In 1859 the Austrians were driven out of northern Italy with the help of France and that part of the country was united. By 1861 all of southern Italy and most of the Papal States were brought in by similar methods. The pope retained only the city of Rome, and only the help of French troops allowed him to maintain that.

The final blow came in 1870. When war broke out between France and Prussia, the French troops were recalled from Rome and the Italian kingdom seized the city and made it its capital. Thus was created the difficult "Roman Question." Neither side was completely wrong. Italy without Rome was unthinkable, but at the same time the city had been stolen from the Church and Pius refused to recognize the change. Instead, the pope withdrew to the Vatican, regarding himself as a voluntary prisoner and refusing to recognize the Italian state. Moreover, he forbade Italian Catholics either to vote or hold office in the Italian national government. This was perhaps a mistake, since it enabled the enemies of the Church to completely dominate Italian affairs. For the first time in centuries the pope had lost his temporal power, and in the eyes of a secular world the prestige of the papacy was never lower.

The Spiritual Position of the Papacy. In many ways, although the men of the time did not know it, the loss of the temporal power of the papacy was a blessing in disguise. It enabled the pope to concentrate more on spiritual matters and to become truly international in his outlook. At the same time, the improvements in communications made it possible for the pope to take a more active role in the affairs of the Church throughout the world. Thus, the spiritual power of the papacy became more impressive during the reign of Pius IX.

The Immaculate Conception. Pius had always been devoted to the Blessed Mother and the trials of his pontificate increased this devotion. In fact, devotion to Mary was growing throughout the entire Church. In 1830 Mary appeared to St. Catherine Labouré and from this apparition came the Miraculous Medal. In 1849 Pius asked the bishops of the Church to state their opinions as to the legitimacy of Mary's Immaculate Conception. The replies were overwhelmingly favorable and the pope appointed a commission to investigate the matter. Its report was favorable and on December 8, 1854 the pope proclaimed the dogma of the Immaculate Conception of Our Lady: Mary was conceived free from the taint of original sin.

The declaration of this dogma was important for several reasons. In the first place, it was a clear instance of the soon to be defined power of papal infallibility. Moreover, the fact that Mary was free from original sin reminded all other men that they were subject to it, and this was a stinging rebuke to an unbelieving age that no longer accepted the reality of sin. Finally, Mary herself appeared to St. Bernadette Soubirous at Lourdes in 1858 announcing herself as the Immaculate Conception. The many cures which have taken place at this shrine served to remind the world that all things cannot be explained in terms of matter alone.

The Syllabus of Errors was issued by Pope Pius in 1864. A list of the chief errors of the day, intended to aid the bishops, it was violently attacked by liberals everywhere. Unfortunately the document had been badly edited and a careless reading seemed to indicate that the Church was condemning everything in the modern world. Fortunately, the great French churchman, Bishop Dupanloup, explained the correct meaning of the Syllabus and pointed out that the Church did not condemn true liberty and freedom.

The Vatican Council called by Pius IX assembled on December 8, 1869 and was the first general council since Trent. While the council restated traditional Catholic teaching in opposition to Protestant and liberal errors, its definition of papal infallibility was far more important. Almost all the bishops agreed that this was a truth of the Catholic religion, but some argued that it was not expedient to formally declare it at that time. But after long debate the council finally settled the issue on July 18, 1870. It declared that when the pope speaks *ex cathedra* —that is, when he speaks in his official position, on a matter of faith or morals—he is infallible by the direction of the Holy Spirit and cannot make an error. Except for a small group in Germany, called the "Old Catholics" the faithful enthusiastically accepted this doctrine.

The End of the Reign. Pius IX ruled as pope until 1878. While his policies have been much attacked, he was clearly the right man for the time. If his attitude to the world outside was largely negative, this was necessary so that the truths of the Faith could be defended. He himself knew that a more positive approach would be necessary for his successor. When the casket of Pius was carried toward its final resting place, a fanatic group of Italian Masons attempted unsuccessfully to seize it and throw it into the river. It was the last attack the great pontiff would have to bear from a secular world.

The Reign of Leo XIII

Gioacchino Vincenzo Pecci was elected Pope Leo XIII on February 20, 1878. A saintly and learned man with a pleasing manner, he had had wide experience in the Church before his election. Leo was determined to put his talents to work in order to restore the place of the Church in the world and to bring the wisdom of the Faith to a world in serious need of guidance.

The Kulturkampf. Leo inherited a bad situation in Germany from the reign of Pius IX. Like Italy, Germany was only recently united and its leader, Bismarck, was extremely suspicious of the Catholic Church and the Catholic political party. Thus, he determined to destroy the position of the Church in a campaign which he and his supporters called the *Kulturkampf,* or the "battle for civilization." Priests were forbidden to criticize the government from the pulpit and all candidates for the priesthood were required to spend three years in a state university. Even seminaries were subjected to state inspection. Finally, most religious orders were expelled from the country. But Bismarck's program met the opposition and defiance of the great majority of German Catholics. Moreover, the German leader soon felt the need for Catholic support as the result of the rise of socialism. Making sure not to arouse Bismarck's stubbornness, Leo XIII gradually persuaded him to revoke most of the anti-Catholic legislation. The result was a victory for the Church and an eloquent testimony to the power of loyal Catholics to resist unjust legislation.

The French Attack on the Church.   Leo was not so successful in France. Despite the pope's advice that all French Catholics should support the French Republican government, many Catholics refused to do so and demanded the return of the monarchy. They thus provided the government with a perfect excuse to persecute the Church. After 1880 a long series of anti-clerical laws were passed. The clergy was forced out of hospitals and all charitable institutions. Religious orders were required to obtain authorization from the state or else leave the country. Religious instruction was banned in public and private schools alike. Finally, in 1905 separation of Church and state was declared and all Church property was taken over by the state. This was a serious blow, for it deprived the clergy of most of their support. Yet, out of this persecution sprang a vigorous French Church in the twentieth century.

The Roman Question.   Leo was unable to make any progress with the difficult situation in Italy. Even if the pope had desired a settlement, the Italian government made one impossible. The Church in Italy was subjected to a bitter persecution. All religious orders were banned and their property was confiscated. Anti-Catholic propaganda was encouraged and religion was banned from the schools. Even public worship was put under government control. But if no settlement was possible, Leo wisely refrained from any actions which would have made the situation worse.

Leo and the Encyclicals.   More than anything else, however, Leo is noted as a great teacher. Making use of encyclicals, or letters to the Church, he applied his talents to the instruction of the whole Church.

Many of the pope's encyclicals dealt with the problems of the world. In *Inscrutabili* he attributed the ills of modern civilization to the rejection of God and religion.

157

Immortale Dei laid down Christian principles for the relation between Church and state. The pope pointed out that the Church had no intention of interfering in purely political affairs, but he did demand that the Church should be left free to carry out its spiritual function. *Libertas Praestantissimum* dealt with human liberty. Leo stated that the Church had always defended true freedom, but he warned that there can be no liberty without law, and that the complete rejection of authority would lead only to utter confusion.

The pope also dealt with intellectual matters. *Aeterni Patris* recommended a revival of the philosophy of St. Thomas Aquinas as best suited to the needs of the Church. *Providentissimus Deus* urged the necessity of a careful study of Sacred Scripture. *Saepenumero* contained the pope's views on history. The historian was reminded that the greatest obligation is to tell the truth since, the pope argued, the truth could never harm the Faith.

Spiritual matters also fell within the scope of the pope's teaching. *Arcanum Divinae Sapientiae* laid down the Christian teaching with regard to marriage. Other encyclicals encouraged devotion to the Holy Ghost, the use of the rosary, and consecrated the world to the Sacred Heart of Jesus.

Leo and the Social Problem. The pope also took great interest in the plight of the workers oppressed by the low wages and poor working conditions of the nineteenth century. Fortunately, other Catholics had earlier prepared the way for the pope. In France, Antoine Frédéric Ozanam (1813-53) founded the St. Vincent de Paul Society to care for poor workers. He soon discovered that charity was not enough and demanded social justice for the workers. In Germany, Bishop Wilhelm von Ketteler (1811-77) was very active in behalf of the workers and urged the formation of trade unions to protect their rights.

To such work as this, Pope Leo added his masterful encyclical, *Rerum Novarum*. The pope rejected both the abuses of capitalism and the false solutions of atheistic socialism. Holding that the possession of private property is legitimate, he nevertheless insisted that this ownership is limited and that those who own property have obligations to those who do not. Leo argued that justice demands a fair profit for the employers and fair wage for the workers and that laborers are justified in forming trade unions to secure justice. The pope hoped that employers and workers could peacefully settle their differences, but at the same time he acknowledged that it was the duty of the state to see that none are unjustly treated.

Leo's accomplishments were thus very great, for under his leadership the Church became increasingly respected. Leo made it clear, the secularists to the contrary, that the Church was not opposed to the rightful accomplishments of the modern world and that the Church had much to offer that world.

The Reign of Pius X

In August of 1903 Giuseppe Sarto was elected Pope Pius X. His entire life had been spent in pastoral work and at the time of his election he was the Cardinal-Archbishop of Venice. Born of a poor family, he was a man of the people. Determined to carry on the program of Leo XIII, he took as his motto "to restore all things in Christ."

Pius and Heresy. Before Pius could carry on his positive work, he found it necessary to deal with a threat to the Faith. A small group of men had gone too far with Pope Leo's attempt to reconcile the Church with the modern world. They determined to do this by sacrificing many of the Faith's eternal truths in order to make Christianity more acceptable to modern ears. This heresy came to be known as *modernism*. Under the leadership

159

of such men as Fathers Loisy of France and Tyrrell of England, the modernists depreciated dogma and held that each individual could hold his own truth. Moreover, they insisted that pious living was more important than religious truth. Pius saw the danger of such teachings and in 1907 the encyclical *Lamentabili* condemned modernism as "the synthesis of all heresies." Moreover, the pope took vigorous steps to make sure that no one in charge of souls or concerned with the preparation of candidates for the priesthood held such ideas and recommended the study of St. Thomas Aquinas to refute such errors. Fortunately, the great majority of those involved submitted to the judgement of the papacy.

The reforms of Pius X were numerous. A thorough reorganization of the Papal Curia was carried out and the following bureaus became especially important: The Congregation of the Holy Office took care of all matters pertaining to faith and morals. The Consistorial Congregation was responsible for the appointment of bishops and other Church officials, while the Congregation of the Propagation watched over world-wide missionary activity. The Congregation of the Sacraments dealt with all matters relating to the sacraments. Clerical discipline was the concern of the Congregation of the Council. Finally, the Tribunal of the Rota was given charge of all difficult questions, especially marriage cases. Pius did not rest, however, with this reorganization of the Curia for he also promoted a vigorous and badly needed reform and codification of Canon Law.

The pope was also responsible for numerous other reforms. Priests and all religious were reminded of their duty to instruct the young in the truths of Christianity. A reform of the breviary was affected, and Biblical studies were encouraged by the establishment of a Biblical Institute in Rome. There was also a reform of Church music and the use of Gregorian Chant was made obligatory. Finally, Pius strongly encouraged the frequent and even daily reception of Holy Communion, and ordered that children should receive their first communion as soon as they reached the age of reason.

Pius the Saint.   Pius died late in 1914 just after the First World War broke out, a war he had tried to prevent. He had not succeeded in solving the difficult situation in Italy, or in reversing the anti-clerical policies of the French government. But his reign was one of great value. His numerous reforms and great leadership won wide respect for the Church. But Pius was more than a great administrator. He was also a saint. His holy life set an example for the entire Church and led to his canonization in 1954.

The Missions of the Nineteenth Century

The period after the French Revolution saw a great revival of missionary activity. This revival was primarily due to the impressive recovery of the Church after the revolution, but the activities of European countries also played a part. During the nineteenth century there was a great resurgence of European imperialism. Colonies were established throughout Asia and Africa and these opened the way for missionary activity.

Missionary supporters were many and the papacy continued to vigorously foster evangelization. The old religious orders, especially the restored Jesuits, were active and new missionary orders were founded. In France, Cardinal Lavigerie established the *Missionaries of Our Lady in Africa,* known as the White Fathers, and a similar order of nuns, called the White Sisters, to aid in the work. In Germany, Father Arnold Janssen founded the *Society of the Divine Word* which was active everywhere, even among American negroes. In England, Cardinal Vaughan began a Foreign Missionary College and the *Mill Hill Society,* as it was called, contributed great numbers of priests to the work. Finally, Father Walsh in the United States was instrumental in the founding of the *American Society for Foreign Missions*—the so-called Maryknolls—which includes both priests and nuns.

Lay participation was an important part of missionary work. Numerous societies were formed throughout Europe which required their members both to pray and to contribute to the missions. The best known of these is the *Society for the Propagation of the Faith.* It sprang from a small group established by Pauline Jaricot among the poor working girls in Lyons, France. She first intended only to reform the immoral lives of working girls, but her brother, a student for the priesthood, suggested that the group ought to contribute to the Church's missionary efforts. At first only small sums were collected, but others became interested and the Society was formed. In 1840 Pope Gregory XVI made it a pontifical society. Through the years it provided prayers and funds for the missions throughout the world, and its work was especially helpful in the United States. Moreover, the Society and other similar groups served to emphasize the fact that the missions were not the concern of the clergy alone, for Christ had commanded all his followers to actively spread the Faith.

Missionary problems were, however, serious. Most of the missionaries went into areas that had been colonized by European powers. Quite often the natives resented this foreign control and often transferred their resentment to the Christian Faith. This made conversion difficult and the task was made even worse by some missionaries who unwisely continued to identify the Faith with European culture. Moreover, a very few of the missionaries conducted themselves in a thoroughly childish fashion by opposing the "intrusion" of other religious orders or clergy from other countries into their "territory." But despite these difficulties, great success was achieved.

The scope of missionary activity was worldwide. In

Africa the missionaries opened up new ground despite immense difficulties and frequent martyrdoms. Both the Mohammedans of the north and the natives of the south felt the impact of the Faith and the way was prepared for an even more vigorous effort in the twentieth century.

There was also great activity in the Far East. Many conversions were made in China despite frequent disorder and government interference. In Japan, missionary activity was resumed and in 1882 the first native Japanese priest of modern times was ordained. In India, too, there was much success, for by 1886 there were some 2,500,000 Catholics in the country and some 1,800 native priests. Other areas in the Far East and the islands of the Pacific also were touched by the Christian Faith.

The Church in Latin America experienced grave difficulties during the nineteenth century. At the beginning of the century almost all of the continent revolted against the control of Spain. Most of the clergy favored these revolutions but the hierarchy opposed them and this damaged the image of the Church in the eyes of many Latin Americans. Moreover, most of the new governments attempted to control the Church, much in the fashion of the former Spanish rulers. As the century progressed these governments frequently fell into the hands of secularists and the Church was often persecuted. When the nineteenth century came to a close, Catholicism remained the nominal Faith of most of Latin America but the Church was in need of a great revival.

The Church in the United States

Perhaps the greatest glory of the missionary work of the nineteenth century was the growth of the Faith in the United States, a land that was strongly Protestant. Until the American Revolution, Catholics suffered legal discrimination, but the Constitution granted religious freedom and most state governments eventually adopted this procedure. Thus the Church in the United States found itself in a much different situation from the Church in Europe. The government rendered no positive help to the Faith, but neither did it interfere with the work of the Church.

The Growth of the Church. Throughout the nineteenth century the Church in America remained under missionary control; its bishops were responsible to the Congregation of the Propaganda. The first bishop was John Carroll of Baltimore, who was raised to that rank in 1789. In the beginning his diocese included the entire territory of the United States. But the Church grew too rapidly for this simple organization, and in 1808 Bishop Carroll became an archbishop with other bishops under him.

Such progress continued, and in 1852 the *First Plenary Council of Baltimore* met to enact canonical legislation for the United States. The council also adopted the Immaculate Conception as the patron feast of the Church in the United States and petitioned Pius IX to define that dogma. Throughout the century, the Church continued to grow. Perhaps a comparison of figures will best serve to bring out this fact. At the time of the American Revolution there were 25,000 Catholics in one diocese. By 1852 this had increased to 2,000,000 Catholics in 34 dioceses, and by 1910 there were 16,000,000 of the faithful in 95 dioceses.

Problems of the American Church. The great rise in the membership of the Church was not, however, primarily due to conversions. Rather, the tremendous flow of immigrants into the country was responsible. This fact was significant because most of the problems of the Church in the United States were somehow connected to the problem of assimilating so many different national groups into one body.

The task of helping the immigrants to adjust to the new ways of America was one of the most difficult problems faced by the Church. Most of the immigrants came from Ireland, Germany, and Italy and they naturally found it hard to live in such a new environment. The Church was thus presented with a great educational task. But there was another problem. Often the children of these immigrants, in their anxiety to be good Americans, went too far and cast off the Faith with the other traditions and customs of the old country. Once again the Church was presented with a difficult task which, however, it was largely able to carry out. Most of the descendants of the immigrants remained loyal to the Faith.

Another difficult problem, known as *trusteeism*, also was involved in the immigrant situation. In the beginning, parish property was often owned and administered by a group of lay trustees. There was nothing inherently wrong with the system, although the present practice of allowing the title of all Church property to remain in the hands of the bishop is preferable. But often these trustees overstepped their authority and interfered in purely ecclesiastical matters, such as the selection of the pastor. Occasionally the appointee of the bishop was refused admittance to the church. This situation became even more serious as the result of national differences. Parishes largely composed of Irishmen, for example, refused to accept French pastors. Stiff resistance on the part of the hierarchy was required before such dangerous practices were repressed.

Finally, the large number of immigrants who made up the Catholic faithful led to prejudice. Most of the immigrants were poor and some more "respectable" Americans looked down on them. Some feared that the large number of Catholic foreigners coming into the United States was a threat to the Protestant and republican traditions of the nation. Organizations arose to do battle with this "Catholic menace." The so-called Know

Nothings of the early nineteenth century later gave way to the American Protective Association. Much propaganda was directed against the Church. A typical example was *The Awful Disclosures of Maria Monk* which purportedly described immoral activity in the convents. At times there was violence. In 1834 a mob burned an Ursuline Convent in Boston under the pretext of "rescuing" a novice. In 1853 a papal envoy to the United States was roughly treated in several cities. But many Americans refused to accept this nonsense. George Washington praised the patriotism of Catholics, and Abraham Lincoln denounced the unreasoning prejudice of many of his countrymen. Moreover, the devoted service of Catholic nuns in caring for the wounded in the Civil War won much respect for the Church. Finally, Cardinal Gibbons, the great American churchman of the later nineteenth century, did much by his writings and example to demonstrate that Catholics were good citizens and loyal to their country. Anti-Catholic prejudice did not cease at the end of the century, but violence against the Church was being confined more and more to the "lunatic fringe."

The accomplishments of the American Church in the nineteenth century were quite impressive. Some converts were won to the Faith. Foremost among these were Orestes Brownson (1803-76) who became a militant Catholic journalist, and Isaac Hecker (1819-88) who founded the *Paulists* to concentrate solely on the conversion of the United States. The Church also produced numerous leaders such as John Carroll and Cardinal Gibbons. A large number of Catholic newspapers were founded for the instruction of the faithful and the Church gave great encouragement to social justice and the rights of the working class.

There was also a considerable growth of the Catholic parish school system and numerous Catholic colleges and universities were established. So great were these achievements that in 1908 Pope Pius X removed the Church in the United States from missionary status. It should not be forgotten, however, that all this progress would not have been possible without help from abroad. The Society for the Propagation of the Faith, for example, contributed over $6,000,000 to the United States in the nineteenth century. This fact should not be forgotten by American Catholics who are today asked to lend their support to the foreign missions.

Religious Life in the Nineteenth Century

The liturgy saw no great changes during the period, but the reforms of Pius X with regard to Church music and the reception of Holy Communion were important. Morever, devotion to the Blessed Mother occupied an extremely important place in the religious life of the people.

Religious Orders. In addition to those devoted to missionary work, other religious orders were established in the nineteenth century. The *Marianists,* founded by William de Chaminade, did much good work in the field of education, as did the *Little Brothers of Mary.* The *Fathers of the Blessed Sacrament* were especially active in fostering devotion among the faithful. Moreover, the older religious orders carried on their good work.

Saints. The chief function of the Church is to produce saints, and seen from this angle the Church was never stronger than it was in the nineteenth century, for the number of saints and near-saints was as great as in any preceding era. Only a few of the more prominent ones can be mentioned here. St. John Bosco was noted for his care of the poor and especially his concern for young boys. St. John Baptist Vianney, the curé of Ars, set a worthy example for all parish priests, despite his only

167

mediocre intellectual ability. St. Theresa of Lisieux, the "Little Flower," was noted for her charity and devotion to Christ.

The growth of lay participation was probably the outstanding fact in the religious life of the century. Everywhere the laity took a more active part in the Church, defending it in the intellectual world, and participating in missionary work. Morever, the coming of democracy made it only natural that the laity should play a larger role. This trend was happily realized by Pius X in the great encouragement which he gave to Catholic Action. Laymen were warned that prayer was not enough. They were asked to participate in the work of the Church, under the direction of the hierarchy. Laymen were to put their knowledge of the world at the service of the Church, and to bring their knowledge of the Faith to the service of the world.

Conclusion

The story of the Church in the nineteenth century is thus a very difficult and complex one. On the one hand the Church underwent constant attacks and the papacy was deprived of its temporal authority. But on the other hand, the Church demonstrated tremendous vigor. The last half of the century saw three great popes, each of whom was well suited to the needs of his time. There were many saints, vigorous missionary activity, and an attempt to bring the wisdom of the Faith to bear on the problems of the world. In short, if the Church still lived in a hostile world, that world was nonetheless beginning to pay a grudging respect to the "Bark of St. Peter."

STUDY QUESTIONS

1. Point out the areas in the Church's life during the nineteenth century where you think you can find the

grace of the Spirit of Christ at work. Give reasons for your convictions.

2. What considerations, humanly speaking, should have prevented the growth of the Church during this century?

3. To what aspect of the gospel of Christ did the Church of the nineteenth century bear strong witness? Explain.

4. No century or civilization is born Christian but must be "baptized." What elements of the nineteenth century did the Church have to win over for Christ?

5. In what sense could the loss of the Papal States be called providential?

6. What events took place in the Body of Christ during the nineteenth century which seem to have been the greatest good for the spread of the gospel?

7. What did Christ do for His Bride, the Church, during the nineteenth century that fulfilled His intention expressed in Eph. 5:26-27?

BIBLIOGRAPHY

BURTON, KATHERINE. *Difficult Star: The Life of Pauline Jaricot.* (New York: 1947).

(A good biography of the founder of the Society for the Propagation of the Faith.)

CORRIGAN, RAYMOND. *The Church and the Nineteenth Century.* (Milwaukee: 1938).

(A good study of the Church in a difficult century.)

ELLIS, JOHN TRACY. *American Catholicism.* (Chicago: 1956).

(A short history of the American Church.)

FULOP-MILLER, RENÈ. *Leo XIII and Our Times.* (New York: 1937).

(A good biography of a great pope.)

HALES, E. E. Y. *The Catholic Church in the Modern World.* (New York: 1958).

(A good and readable summary of the history of the Church in the nineteenth and twentieth centuries.)

————. *Pio Nono*. (New York: 1954).
(A good biography of Pope Pius IX.)

MAYNARD, THEODORE. *The Story of American Catholicism*.
(New York: 1941).
(A very capable survey of the history of the American
Church.)

NEILL, THOMAS P. *They Lived the Faith*. (Milwaukee: 1951).
(This work contains interesting studies of some of the most
important lay leaders in the nineteenth century Church.)

Chapter VIII

The Contemporary Church

Christ Remains Faithful to His "Bride"

Introduction

THE Church of the nineteenth century grew strong in spite of determined secularist opposition. The Church of the twentieth century has achieved an even more impressive record in this regard. Despite the onslaught of two disastrous world wars and the attacks of the totalitarian Fascist and Communist systems, the Church has continued to grow in strength. Great popes have extended missionary activity, better adapted the Church to the modern world, and fostered the growing participation of the laity in the work of the Church.

The World of the Twentieth Century

It is always difficult to describe the major trends of an age, and this difficulty is further increased when the period under discussion is one in which the historian finds himself living. Yet some attempt must be made to indicate briefly the major forces of the twentieth century.

The decreasing power of Europe has been one of the most outstanding factors of our age. Despite vigorous recovery, two long and terrible wars have taken their toll. Moreover, it is important to note that in both of these wars it was a non-European nation, the United States, that held the balance of power. The influence of Europe has been further compromised by the revolutions in former colonial areas. European imperialism has definitely come to an end. Thus a new world has come into being. It is a world which has accepted many of the ideas of European civilization, but it has interpreted these ideas in terms of its own culture. This fact presents the Church with a compelling challenge. It must somehow convert this world, and to do so it must finally demonstrate that Christianity is not merely a European or even a Western development. The Faith must be shown to be world-wide and universal, as Christ intended it to be. Great effort will be required to achieve this, however, since the Church has so long been identified with Europe and the Americas.

Unprecedented Material Achievements. The scientific and technological revolutions of the modern world have produced great material advancements. Sicknesses have been cured, the life span has been lengthened, industry has provided numerous and cheaper products for everyday life, and means of transportation and communication have been greatly improved and speeded up. All these things have produced a better life, but they have also brought a more complex world. Seen from a religious point of view, these things can be either good or bad. Often the better life leads to an unrestricted search for pleasure. Yet, while mortification may be a good thing, the continued existence of human misery is hardly a

Christian ideal. Similarly, new means of communication can lead to the spread of moral evil, but they can also be put at the disposal of the Faith. It is the duty of every Christian, therefore, to make proper use of the achievements of the modern world.

The rise of totalitarianism has been the most important political and economic fact of the century. Totalitarianism may be defined as a way of life and a system of government in which the state controls every phase of human activity. Rejecting the Christian view that the state is the servant of the individual, it teaches the contrary doctrine that the individual exists for the good of the state. The two major types of totalitarianism have been *Communism* and *Fascism-Nazism*. The theories behind them are quite different, but both equally result in the enslavement of man. Fascism subjects the nation to the will of a single leader (*Il Duce* or *Der Führer*), whereas Communism subjects all to the dictatorship of the Party. Fascism teaches the superiority of a nation and Communism advocates the superiority of a class. Both reject God and any claims of religion upon the hearts and minds of men. Both have been ruthless persecutors of the Church.

Increasing violence has therefore been a dominant theme of the twentieth century. Two devastating world wars have been fought, and a third is threatened. Moreover, these have been total wars in which civilian populations have been subjected to unlimited misery. This constant war and disruption have gravely damaged the Church and have impeded its work. Yet, it may perhaps serve a good cause. While it is not necessary to believe that God directly sends such wars to chastise the people, such violence nonetheless inevitably flows from sin. The realization of this truth may yet lead souls back to God.

Intellectually, the twentieth century has been an age of increasing despair. Men, taught by the ideas of the modern world to expect an earthly paradise, have discovered that these ideas have failed to produce it. But even this despair may prove a healthy thing if it can turn man back to the realization of his need for God.

Thus, the Church of the twentieth century faces a complex situation. On the one hand it is menaced by evil forces; on the other, there is the possibility that the Church may be able to turn the forces of the modern world to its service and thereby fulfill its missions.

The Papacy and Europe

In the late summer of 1914 World War I began. The excessive nationalism of the nineteenth century thus bore its evil fruit. The Church and the world were presented with an ominous warning of what the twentieth century would bring. Fortunately, the Faith found great leaders to guide her in these difficult years.

Pope Benedict XV (1914-22) had to grapple with the problems of the war throughout his reign. Giacomo della Chiesa was an excellent choice for the papacy. Possessing wide experience in papal diplomacy as Assistant Secretary of State, he had been the Archbishop of Bologna for seven years. Benedict did not take sides in the war; instead he worked hard to procure peace. His first encyclical, *Ad Beatissimi*, traced the cause of the war to the rejection of Christian values and pleaded for peace. When violations of the laws of war occurred, the pope was the first to protest.

But Benedict did not merely protest. Although his advice was not followed, he attempted to mediate the conflict and bring about peace. Moreover, he tried to lessen the cruelty of the war. Papal money flowed into devastated areas to aid the distressed populations. A Prisoners of War Bureau was established in the Vatican which improved conditions in many camps and notified families of the status of missing relatives. When the war finally ended, the pope pleaded for understanding on all sides so that a world of justice and charity could be built. When Benedict died in 1922 he had won the respect of most of the world for his works of charity and advocacy of peace.

Pope Pius XI (1922-39) was faced with the great problems of the inter-war years. Achille Ratti was born of a middle class family in 1857 and was ordained to the priesthood in 1879. A learned man, he spent a quiet life until the age of sixty when he was appointed the papal nuncio to Poland. In 1921 he became the Cardinal-Archbishop of Milan and the following year he was elected to the papacy. A very active pope, he was greatly interested in the problem of peace and he took as his motto: "The peace of Christ through the reign of Christ." But he expressed the fear in *Ubi Arcano Dei* that the world was heading to another and more serious struggle. That war did not come until 1939, but the Church was faced by innumerable problems in the intervening years.

The settlement of the Roman question was perhaps the greatest achievement of Pius XI. In 1922 the Fascist party under the leadership of Benito Mussolini seized power in Italy. Mussolini was certainly no practicing Catholic, but he did see the need of restoring order in Italy and he knew that a reconciliation with the papacy would greatly increase his popularity. Thus, when the Facist government took several steps favorable to the Church, Pius proved ready to meet it half way. In August of 1926 unofficial talks got underway and these soon led to official negotiations between Mussolini and Cardinal Gasparri.

The result was the *Lateran Treaty* in February, 1929. Italy recognized that the pope was the political sovereign of tiny Vatican City, and thus the independence of the papacy was assured. In turn, Pius acknowledged the national government of Italy and accepted its possession of Rome and the Papal States. Italy also agreed to pay

175

the pope a large indemnity for his territorial leases. Attached to this treaty was a concordat between the papacy and Italy to define the position of the Church in that country. Catholicism was declared the official religion of the state, religion was taught in all schools, and the Catholic regulations on marriage were given sanction in civil law. The stormy Roman question was finally settled. Unfortunately, however, the Fascist state soon began to attack the Church.

Conflict with Fascist Italy broke out over the question of education. Mussolini was determined to use the Italian schools for propaganda in order to produce good Fascists. The Church naturally resisted such a program. When Mussolini attempted to quell all Catholic youth organizations, and attacked Catholic Action groups, the papacy replied. In *Non Abbiamo Bisogno* Pius defended the need for liberty and denounced Fascism as a pagan worship of the state. Mussolini desperately needed Catholic support and backed down from his program. Thereafter, a shaky truce prevailed until Mussolini was overthrown in the Second World War.

The Conflict with Nazism. In 1933 a more extreme and violent brand of Fascism came into power in Germany. Nazism, as it was called, was led by Adolph Hitler who proclaimed his aim to dominate Europe. Hitler had little use for religion, and immediately attempted to control the Protestant churches in Germany. With regard to the Catholics, however, he moved more slowly. In 1933 Eugenio Pacelli, the future Pius XII, negotiated what appeared to be a satisfactory concordat with the Nazi government.

But as Hitler solidified his power, he turned on the Church. Real persecution began in 1935. Catholic Action was destroyed, young people were forced into Nazi youth organizations, violent propaganda was allowed to circulate against the Faith, religious instruction was driven from the schools, religious orders were banned, and many of the clergy were arrested. By 1937 Pius could tolerate such violence no longer and he replied with *Mit Brennender Sorge,* denouncing the racism and excessive nationalism of the Nazi regime. But the persecution continued and the war brought on by the Nazis caused the Church further suffering.

The Civil War in Spain. In Spain the Church was presented with a serious threat from leftist, anti-clerical forces. Spain had always been a Catholic country, but unfortunately the Church had lost touch with the great mass of the people. Social inequality and widespread poverty turned many away from the Faith. When a Republic was established after the overthrow of King Alfonso XIII in 1931, secularist liberals and socialists immediately began a persecution of the Church. Church property was confiscated, and religious orders were suppressed. However, frequent acts of violence occurred, and the government did little to protect Catholic churches. Pius condemned these outrages in 1933 with *Dilectissima Nobis.* But the persecution did not end and in 1936 the army, led by General Francisco Franco, revolted against the republican government. Most Catholics immediately came to the support of Franco, and a long civil war followed. Acts of unspeakable cruelty were committed by both sides. Franco finally achieved victory in 1939, and the Church was restored to its former position. The threat from the left was thus stopped but Franco's regime, although perhaps necessary, has remained completely dictatorial.

Peace in the Democracies. In contrast to the violent attacks of the totalitarian states the Church was able to lead a fairly peaceful life in the Western democracies. In France the old anti-clerical laws were not generally enforced. The result has been a strong and vibrant

177

Church which has made important intellectual contributions to the Faith. In England also the Church was left free, and numerous conversions have resulted.

Pius XII (1939-58). When Pius XI died in February of 1939, the great world war he had tried so hard to prevent was only months away. But his reign was certainly not a failure on that account. His fearless resistance to totalitarian tyranny won the respect of the whole world. The new pope was even more respected and loved. Eugenio Pacelli was born of a distinguished Roman family in 1876 and became a priest in 1899. His rise in the clerical life was rapid. After extensive diplomatic experience, he was named a cardinal in 1929, and became the papal Secretary of State in 1930. His election to the papacy in 1939 was universally hailed as a wise choice.

World War II occupied the early part of his reign. Even before the struggle began, Pius worked to preserve peace by prayer, appeals to rulers, and diplomatic activity. During the war the pope was responsible for many works of mercy. The Pontifical Relief Commission sent food and supplies to all devastated areas that could be reached. Refugees were cared for and conditions in the prison camps were improved wherever governments would allow the papacy to take action. Moreover, Pius identified himself with suffering victims of the war. Despite danger, he refused to leave Rome and could often be seen in the streets caring for the sick and wounded. When the war ended in 1945, Pius had again demonstrated the universal charity of the Church.

The Threat of Communism. After the war, Pius XII was anxious to reconstruct the Church on a world-wide basis, but many of his plans were hampered by the power of Communist Russia. Communism came to Russia in 1917 under the leadership of Nicolai Lenin, but fortunately its power was confined to that country for several years. Even so, the Church was aware of the threat of this totalitarian system, for in 1937 Pius XI published *Divini Redemptoris* to warn the faithful of the dangers of atheistic Communism. But after World War II Russia emerged as a world power and successfully dominated many central and eastern European countries.

Everywhere the result has been the same: persecution. Anti-Christian policies are an inherent part of the Communist system, and Christianity has been persecuted in Russia since 1917. After the war this was extended to all the conquered countries. In Poland, a strongly Catholic country, the Church has survived only by the narrowest of margins. In Hungary, Cardinal Mindszenty was thrown into prison when he resisted Communist attacks on Catholic education. In Czechoslovakia, various members of the hierarchy were arrested and many priests were killed. Of the estimated 425 million Catholics in the world some 53 million found themselves under Communist domination.

At every opportunity, Pius XII denounced the Communist persecution of the Church and warned the Catholics of democratic countries to be on their guard. Moreover, the coming of the "cold war" led him to fear that the threat to world peace was most serious. The power of Communism was still strong when Pius XII died in the fall of 1958. Perhaps the greatest of the twentieth century popes, his passing was mourned by the entire free world.

Pope John XXIII (1958-63) may well rank as the most beloved and respected pope of the twentieth century, despite the brevity of his reign. Angelo Guiseppe Roncali was born of poor parents in 1881, ordained a priest in 1904, and saw long service in papal diplomacy before he became the Cardinal-Archbishop of Venice. His election to the papacy in October of 1958 was something of a surprise, for he was not a pre-election favorite. But in spite of his advanced age at the time of the election, Pope John proved a most active and vigorous pontiff. His reign was marked by innovation, and by a spirit of making the Church and its message more meaningful to the men of the twentieth century.

The pope was very interested in the betterment of living conditions for all men throughout the world, and often spoke and wrote on this topic. He was also a devoted champion of world peace. While he was not unaware of the evils of Communism, he none the less hoped to improve relations between the Vatican and the communist regimes. It was perhaps for this reason that he granted a private audience to Alexie Adzhubei, the editor of the communist newspaper *Izvestia*, and the son-in-law of Premier Khrushchev.

Pope John was vitally interested in the ecumenical movement of the twentieth century and received many non-Catholic religious leaders during his papacy. His meeting with the Archbishop of Canterbury, the Primate of the Anglican Church, was typical of these meetings. The pope also met with many non-Christian religious leaders. John XXIII realized that religious unity was a very difficult undertaking and that it would take a long time. But he hoped that his policies would ease the way for future progress. Moreover, the pope believed that all religions have much in common and that by working together they could greatly influence the world for good.

Perhaps the greatest contribution of Pope John was his convocation of the *Second Vatican Council* to reform and update the Church. The work of the council, which first met in 1962, was far along when John XXIII died in June of 1963. His kindness and progressive policies won him widespread respect, and his passing was mourned by the entire world. It is certain that his influence on the Church will continue for many years.

Pope Paul VI (1963-   ) has shown his determination to continue the policies inaugurated by Pope John. Giovanni Battista Montini was born in 1897, the son of a progressive Italian lawyer and journalist. He entered the seminary at an early age, and then served long years in the papal diplomatic service. After holding a high diplomatic office under Pope Pius XII, he was named Archbishop of Milan where he had much success in winning the workers back to the Church. His good work at Milan earned him a cardinal's hat from John XXIII, and he became a close adviser of the pope. Unlike Pope John, his election came as no surprise, and he was named pope in one of the shortest conclaves of the twentieth century. Pope Paul has declared that the two chief aims of his pontificate are the attainment of peace and Christian unity, and in conformity with these aims, he declared that Vatican Council II, begun by Pope John, would be continued.

Summary. The great popes of the twentieth century have thus successfully defended the Church and made it strong in the face of totalitarian opposition. But their activities have not been purely political. The spiritual measures promoted by these pontiffs have been of tremendous significance and will be covered in a later section.

The American Church in the Twentieth Century

The Church in the United States truly became mature in the twentieth century. Overcoming great obstacles, it presented an example of what the Faith could achieve in a free environment.

Anti-Catholic Bigotry, however, continued in the twentieth century. Its most notable proponent was the *Ku Klux Klan,* a secret society which preached hatred of Negroes, Jews, and Catholics. When Governor Alfred E. Smith, a Catholic, ran for president in 1928, anti-Catholic feeling reached serious proportions. All kinds of outrageous charges were made and even well-meaning Protestants were affected. Smith was defeated, although it should be pointed out that he probably would have lost even if he had not been a Catholic, for 1928 was clearly a Republican year.

Bigotry died down to some extent after the election, but incidents continued to occur. President Truman's attempt to send a personal representative to the Vatican was voted down in the Senate as a result of anti-Catholic pressure. Bigotry enjoyed another upswing in the 1960 presidential campaign, but the election of John F. Kennedy ended forever the myth that a Catholic was not fit to occupy the highest office in the land. Anti-Catholic feeling is still by no means dead, but it is losing its force, and is mostly confined to ignorant people.

The growth of the Church in the United States has been amazing. In 1955 there were some 32,500,000 Catholics in this country served by some 46,970 priests. Catholics made up about 20 per cent of the population and were the largest single religious denomination.

The Maturity of the Church. The growth of the American Church has not only been one of quantity; there has also been an increase in quality. A rising number of vocations to the religious life has been an encouraging sign. American contributions to the missions have been large. In 1957, 66 per cent of all the money collected by the Propaganda of the Faith was contributed by citizens of the United States. The American Church has also furnished many workers for the foreign missions, and now laymen are engaging in this work.

The National Catholic Welfare Conference, a voluntary association of American bishops, has done much to improve Catholic Action, and has consistently advocated a sane view on controversial public questions. The Church has made great use of radio and television in spreading the word of God, and worthy Catholic journals and newspapers have appeared. The lay journal *Commonweal*, the Jesuit publication *America*, and the diocesan *St. Louis Review* may be taken as three good examples of Catholic journalism.

Moreover, the Church has played an important role in

the affairs of this country. Social justice has been consistently advocated, and the Church has actively supported the Negro in his search for equality. In 1947 the Cardinal-Archbishop of St. Louis, Joseph E. Ritter, courageously ended segregation in the Catholic schools in his diocese and similar action on the part of the Archbishop of New Orleans indicates that the Church will stand firm on this issue, despite the opposition of some misinformed laymen.

Finally, without any state support, the Catholic school system has grown both in quantity and quality. Yet, one of the great needs of the Church of the United States is for greater intellectual activity on the part of the faithful. If the Church is to fulfill its mission in the United States, it must make more of an impression on the learned world and infuse that world with Christian principles.

The Missions of the Twentieth Century

Papal direction has been of tremendous importance in the missionary work of the Church. As soon as World War I came to an end, Benedict XV turned his attention to the missions, and in 1919 he published *Maximum Illud* to guide missionary activity. Pointing out that it was the duty of every Catholic to support the missions, the pope also warned of the danger of allowing national pride to interfere with the universal mission of the Church. Benedict stressed the need for the development of a native clergy in each mission land and made this the most important task of the missionaries.

These ideas were continually repeated and strengthened by Pius XI. His consecration of six Chinese bishops in 1926 stressed the universal nature of the Church, and his centralization of all missionary funds in Rome led to greater efficiency. Pius especially encouraged the use of medical science in connection with missionary work and mission exhibits aroused the interest of the laity. Pius XII was also greatly interested in the missions. His appointment of a Chinese and an Indian to the College of Cardinals was especially notable. But unfortunately, Pius XII was to see many of his best efforts thwarted by the spread of Communism.

The present status of the missions reveals great progress on the one hand, and the need for greater efforts on the other. In Africa there are 20,000,000 Catholics, 1,700 native priests, and 20 native bishops, but many areas have only been lightly touched by the Faith. In India the Church has remained strong despite government suspicion, but the great mass of the people are still to be reached. In China a growing Church has been persecuted since 1949 by the Communist regime, which has attempted to establish a puppet national Church cut off from Rome. So it is with the missions in other lands. Much has been done, but much yet remains to be accomplished.

The Church in Latin America has experienced great difficulties in the twentieth century. The number of the clergy has been far too small to serve the population, and even the help of Catholics in the United States has not bridged the gap. Moreover, extreme poverty has turned many to Communism and away from the Church. Persecution has resulted in several Latin American countries, most notably in Mexico in the early part of the century and presently in Communist Cuba. Yet, better education and a more active clergy holds promise for a Catholic resurgence.

The importance of the missions for the contemporary Church can hardly be overestimated. Undoubtedly great progress has been made. Yet the serious fact remains that after twenty centuries, a large portion of the world still remains ignorant of the Faith. The Catholic of today must devote even more prayers, money, and time to missionary activity. He must remember that the Church, according to the command of Christ, is essentially a missionary organization. He must remember too that the success of the Church may well depend on the success of the missions, for the non-European nations will play an increasingly important role in the centuries to come.

Religious Life in the Twentieth Century

The twentieth century has seen significant developments in the life of the Church. All these were carried out under the leadership of a papacy which has made use of its wide influence to instruct the faithful by numerous encyclicals. The great concern in all these papal actions is the difficult task of adapting the Church to the modern world, for such adaptation is essential if the Church is to properly carry on its work.

The social problem continued to occupy an important place in papal teaching. In 1931 Pius XI followed up the work of Leo XIII with his own *Quadragesimo Anno*. Pius condemned the abuses of Capitalism and the errors of Communism and suggested a middle approach. The pope pointed out that all men have a social obligation to their neighbor and admitted the necessity of state intervention when employers and workers are unable to settle their differences.

Papal teaching on the social problem was further developed by Pope John XXIII in his *Mater Et Magistra*. Continuing the appeal for social justice, Pope John pointed out that some socialization is entirely permissible if necessary for the welfare of the people. The pope also pleaded that help be given to agriculture and stressed the duty of the more advanced nations to contribute to the welfare of underdeveloped countries. The pope thus demonstrated that justice is not only to be observed within nations, but that it must be followed in international affairs as well.

Pope John also approached the difficult problem of international peace. In *Pacem in Terris* he spoke of the necessity of ending the dangerous arms race and called on all nations to establish a world order based on mutual understanding. He also pleaded for all nations to work together in the interests of achieving a better world for all men. Significantly, the pope addressed this encyclical not just to Catholics, but to all men of good will and most of the present world leaders have praised the pope's message. Thus, once again the relevance of the Faith to the problems of the modern world has been demonstrated.

Other problems of a social nature were also treated in papal encyclicals. With regard to education, Pius XI issued *Divini Illius Magistri* in 1929. The pope reminded parents that they are primarily responsible for the education of their children, and warned that no education could be successful if it neglected the spiritual aspect of man. Pius XI also dealt with marriage in his *Casti Connubii*. The pope pointed out that marriage properly belongs to the care of the Church, because of its sacramental nature, and condemned such abuses as divorce and birth control.

The liturgy was reformed in several important respects. Pius XII was especially active and took many steps to increase the role of the laity in the worship of the Church. Fasting requirements for Communion were reduced in order to facilitate frequent reception of the sacrament. Evening masses were allowed, and the Holy Week ritual was altered so as to make it more meaningful. In 1960 Pope John carried out a further revision of the mass. Moreover, the increasing use of the dialogue mass has served to heighten the value of divine worship.

Dogma has been the subject of several important developments in the twentieth century. In 1943 Pope Pius XII issued *Mystici Corporis* to explain that the Church was truly the Mystical Body of Christ in which all the faithful share. Even more striking, however, was his infallible definition of the Assumption of the Blessed Mother into heaven. Devotion to Mary was also fostered by the activities of the Marian Year in 1954, and such devotion has remained extremely important in the religious life of the Church.

The place of the laity has been repeatedly emphasized by the modern papacy. Pius XI took great interest in Catholic Action and stated that its most important aim was to bring Christian principles to bear on the problems of the age. He warned, however, of the necessity of episcopal direction in such efforts. In line with current developments, Pius XII carefully outlined the place of women in the modern world. It is further expected that the present council will more carefully define the place of the laity in the Church.

An intellectual revival has occupied an important place in the history of the contemporary Church. Great work has been accomplished in such fields as philosophy, theology, Sacred Scripture, and Church history. Occasionally, mistakes have been made and in 1950 Pius XII issued *Humani Generis* to warn against the sacrificing of Christian truth in order to make the Faith more acceptable to unbelievers. This warning was accepted in the proper spirit by almost all Catholics and continued progress has been the result.

The possibility of reunion with dissident sects has also occupied much papal attention. The challenges of the modern world have made all Christians recognize their common heritage and have encouraged the search for unity. Pope John was especially interested in this important matter, and the visit of the Anglican Archbishop of Canterbury to the Vatican in 1960 was symbolic of increased understanding. The present council shows great interest in the possibility of eventual reunion. But the road to unity will not be an easy one, and the Church cannot sacrifice divine truth, no matter how much such a sacrifice might improve the chances for unity. It is the duty, however, of every Catholic to pray and work for the day when there will be one flock and one shepherd.

The Second Vatican Council may very well prove to be the most important single event in the religious life of the twentieth century. Summoned by Pope John XXIII, it is dealing with a multitude of important questions centering around the problem of the Church's adaptation to the modern world. The Holy Father said that while unity of the Christian churches was not the immediate object of the council, he hoped that it would be a step in the direction of that ideal. Pope Paul VI announced, when he was elected pope, that he intended to have the council pursue these same objectives.

Conclusion

Twenty centuries lie behind today's Church, and the flame lit by the Holy Spirit on that first Pentecost has remained bright and grown stronger. At times it flickered and grew dim, but it never went out. The promise of Christ not to abandon His Church has been amply fulfilled, despite human errors and vigorous attacks against the Mystical Body of Christ. The Catholic can indeed look back with satisfaction on the history of the Church.

But satisfaction is not enough, for the future lies ahead. It is a future dark with difficulties and yet bright with promise. The Church finds itself today in a position not unlike the place it occupied in the early days of its existence—but now not on a Mediterranean but rather a world-wide scale. You will remember that the early Church was despised and persecuted throughout the Roman world. It grew strong in the cities, and then when toleration was granted it flourished tremendously and soon most people in the Roman Empire had adopted the Faith.

Today, centuries of secularism have produced a world in confusion. It is possible that man is beginning to realize, in the midst of the violence and despair of the twentieth century, that human happiness cannot be achieved if God is rejected. If such be the case, the Church today might stand on the threshold of a glorious day when its light can shine in every corner of the world. It is the duty of every Catholic, each in his own way and according to his own talents, to carry his light of the Faith into the world and to bring the good news of the Gospel to a world which has desperate need of it.

STUDY QUESTIONS

1. Christ is not just the Founder of the Church. He is its Savior at the present time. In what events of the present can you see the saving presence of Christ?
2. Has the Kingdom of God on earth experienced a growth or a decline during the twentieth century?
3. How has the temporal order affected the Church during our century?
4. Are there any indications in the present life of the Church that the Lord is carrying out the continuing task of reforming His people? Explain.
5. It is the mission of the Church to restore all things in Christ. Where has the Church been successful in her mission in the twentieth century? Where has she yet to be successful?
6. Name and describe the major movements that are attracting great enthusiasm by the disciples of Christ.
7. It has been said that this is a great period of the history of the Church in which to be living. Why?
8. Would you agree that for a long time the Church has not been in the main stream of human life but that she is now returning to a place of influence and leadership in the history of the world? Why?
9. What are the greatest areas for apostolic labor in the world of today?

Bibliography

Burton, Katherine. *Witness of the Light: The Life of Pope Pius XII.* (New York: 1958).
(A good biography.)

Fontenelle, Monsignor R. *His Holiness Pope Pius XI.* Translated by M. E. Fowler. (London: 1938).
(A good biography.)

Fremantle, Anne. *The Papal Encyclicals in Their Historical Context.* (New York: 1956).
(The student can find in this book summaries and selections from the most important papal pronouncements of the last two centuries.)

Giordani, Igino. *Pius X, a Country Priest.* (Milwaukee: 1954).
(A good biography.)

Millot, Renè-Pierre. *Missions in the World Today.* Translated by J. Holland Smith. (New York: 1961).
(A good summary of the status of the Church's missionary work in the twentieth century.)

General
Bibliography

The Catholic Encyclopedia. 15 vols. (New York: 1907).
   (Different articles in this encyclopedia may be consulted for
   almost any aspect of Church history, for points of doctrine,
   and for short biographies of important figures.)
BELLOC, HILAIRE. *The Great Heresies.* (New York: 1938).
   (A short tracing of the major heresies in the history of the
   Church.)
BRUSHER, JOSEPH, S. J. *Popes Through the Ages.* (Princeton:
   1959).
   (A richly illustrated biographical history of the papacy.)
DEWOHL, LOUIS. *Founded on a Rock: A History of the Catholic
   Church.* (Philadelphia: 1961).
   (A very well written work by a very popular Catholic author.)
DEVAULX, BERNARD. *History of the Missions.* Translated by
   Reginald F. Trevitt. (New York: 1961).
   (A good short summary.)
DUNNEY, REV. JOSEPH A. *Church History in the Light of the
   Saints.* (New York: 1944).
   (Contains short accounts of many of the most important
   saints in the history of the Church and relates their lives to
   general developments in the Church.)
EBERHARDT, NEWMAN C. *A Summary of Catholic History.* 2
   vols. (St. Louis: 1961-62).

(An excellent general history of the Church, primarily intended for the use of seminary students. If the student does not wish to completely read this work it is still useful for purposes of reference.)

GRANDI, DOMENICO AND GALLI, ANTONIO. *Story of the Church.* Edited by John Chapin. (New York: 1961).

(A good general study.)

HUGHES, PHILIP. *A Popular History of the Catholic Church.* (New York: 1952).

(A short but useful work by an eminent Catholic historian.)

NEILL, THOMAS P., MCGARRY, DANIEL D., AND HOHL, CLARENCE L. *A History of Western Civilization.* (Milwaukee: 1962).

(A good survey of European history which is very useful for the background of the history of the Church.)

NEILL, THOMAS P. AND SCHMANDT, RAYMOND H. *History of the Catholic Church.* (Milwaukee: 1957).

(A solid and readable Church history.)

RAEMERS, REV. SIDNEY A. *Church History.* (St. Louis: 1936).

(A short history primarily intended for high school students.)

RICE, EDWARD. *The Church: A Pictorial History.* (New York: 1961).

(A very interesting work containing numerous illustrations and pictures set in the framework of a short summary of Church history.)